Teaching Aid Masters

THE UNIVERSITY OF CHICAGO SCHOOL MATHEMATICS PROJECT

PRECALCULUS AND DISCRETE MATHEMATICS

INTEGRATED MATHEMATICS

Includes Teacher's-Edition Warm-ups, grids, charts, graphs, and examples

ISBN: 0-673-45920-9

1 2 3 4 5 6—ML—01 00 99 98

Scott Foresman
Addison Wesley

Editorial Offices: Glenview, Illinois • Menlo Park, California
Sales Offices: Reading, Massachusetts • Atlanta, Georgia
Glenview, Illinois • Carrollton, Texas • Menlo Park, California

http://www.sf.aw.com

Contents

*References in parentheses indicate the first lesson for which the Teaching Aid may be used.

Warm-up

Lesson 1-1

Let $p(x)$ be $3x + 5 \geq 8x - 2$.

1. Is $p(x)$ a statement?
2. Give the value of $p(1)$.
3. Find a value of x for which $p(x)$ is not true.
4. Describe the set of all values of x for which $p(x)$ is true.
5. Describe the set of all values of x for which $p(x)$ is false.

Warm-up

Lesson 1-2

1. Give the opposite of each term.
   - **a.** black
   - **b.** large
   - **c.** positive
   - **d.** 11
   - **e.** wrong
2. Give the negation of each statement.
   - **a.** The color of that car is black.
   - **b.** That is a large triangle.
   - **c.** The solution to the sentence is a positive number.
   - **d.** $x = 11$
   - **e.** You answered all of the questions wrong.

Warm-up

Lesson 1-3

In 1–6, tell whether the sentence is true or false when $x = 30$.

1. $x \geq 30$

2. $x > 30$ and $x = 30$.

3. $x > -31$ and $x < 31$.

4. $x < -31$ and $x > 31$.

5. $x^2 > 900$

6. $x^2 \leq 30x$

7. Give the negation of each sentence in 1–6 and tell whether the negation is true or false when $x = 30$.

Warm-up

Lesson 1-4

1. Make a table showing all possibilities for opening or not opening a door with two locks that are unlocked or locked.

2. Relate the situation in *Warm-up* Question 1 to a truth table.

Warm-up

Lesson 1-5

First determine whether the sentence is a statement. If so, tell whether it is true or false.

1. If $3 > 2$, then $5 > 4$.

2. If $x > 3$, then $x > 4$.

3. For all x, if $x > 3$, then $x > 4$.

Warm-up

Lesson 1-6

Order these statements to put together a logical argument and state its conclusion.

A. If a convex polygon has seven sides, then it is a heptagon.

B. If the sum of the measures of the interior angles of a convex polygon is 900°, then the polygon must have at least 4 obtuse angles.

C. If a convex polygon has seven vertices, then it has 7 sides.

D. If a convex polygon is a heptagon, then the sum of the measures of its interior angles is 900°.

Warm-up

Lesson 1-7

Consider these statements:

All *A*s are *B*s.

Some *B*s are *C*s.

All *C*s are *D*s.

Is it valid to conclude Some *A*s are *D*s? Why or why not?

Warm-up

Lesson 1-8

Let line segments $\overline{AB}$ and $\overline{CD}$ intersect at point *E*.

1. Prove: If *E* is the midpoint of both $\overline{AB}$ and $\overline{CD}$, then lines $\overleftrightarrow{AC}$ and $\overleftrightarrow{BD}$ are parallel.
2. Express the statement to be proved in *Warm-up* Question 1 as a universal conditional.

Definitions from the Lesson

Definition

Let *S* be a set and *p(x)* a property that may or may not hold for any element *x* of *S*. A **universal statement** is a statement of the form

For all x in S, p(x).

or symbolically

$\forall$ *x in S, p(x).*

A universal statement is true if and only if *p(x)* is true for every element *x* in *S*; otherwise, it is **false.**

Definition

Given a universal statement

$\forall$ *x in S, p(x),*

a value of *x* in *S* for which *p(x)* is false is called a **counterexample** to the statement.

Definition

Suppose that *S* is a set and that *p(x)* is a property that may or may not hold for elements *x* of *S*. An **existential statement** is a statement of the form

There exists x in S such that p(x).

or, symbolically,

$\exists$ *x in S such that p(x).*

An existential statement is true if and only if *p(x)* is true for at least one element *x* in *S*, otherwise, it is **false.**

Truth Tables

Truth Table for Negation

p	$-p$
T	F
F	T

Truth Table for *and*

p	q	p *and* q
T	T	T
T	F	F
F	T	F
F	F	F

Truth Table for *or*

p	q	p *or* q
T	T	T
T	F	T
F	T	T
F	F	F

Truth Table for Conditional

p	q	*if* p*, then* q $p \Rightarrow q$
T	T	T
T	F	F
F	T	T
F	F	T

Question 22

	sports teams						foreign language club				fine arts club			academic club		
	football	basketball	baseball	soccer	track	swimming	French	German	Russian	Spanish	drama	chorus	band	math	debate	science
Dominique						✔		✔						✔		
Raul	✔			✔							✔			✔	✔	
Karen					✔		✔						✔	✔		
Tom			✔						✔					✔	✔	✔

Example 1 and Additional Example 1

Example 1

p	q	p and q	not (p and q)	not p	not q	(not p) or (not q)
T	T					
T	F					
F	T					
F	F					

Additional Example 1

p	q	not q	not (p and (not q))	not p	(not p) or q
T	T				
T	F				
F	T				
F	F				

p	q	
T	T	
T	F	
F	T	
F	F	

Logic Networks for Examples 1-3

Example 1

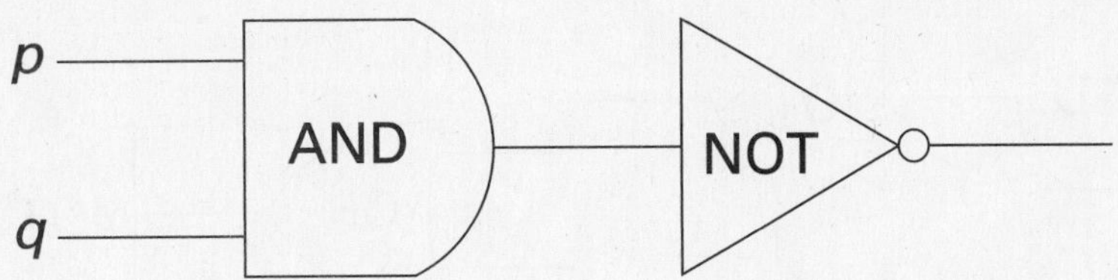

Example 2

p
q
AND
NOT
≡
p
NOT
q
NOT
OR

Example 3

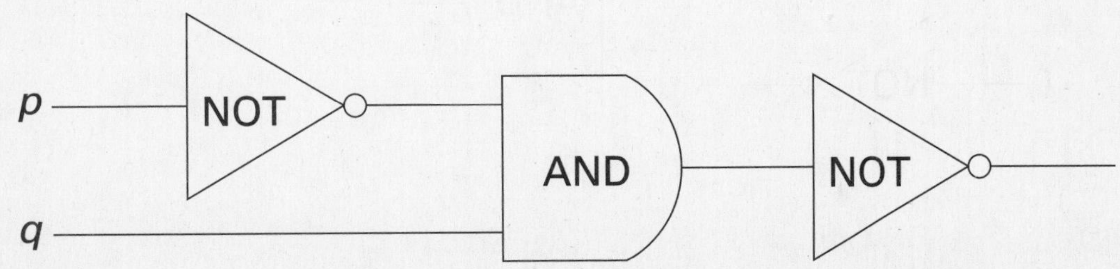

Questions 4-6

4.

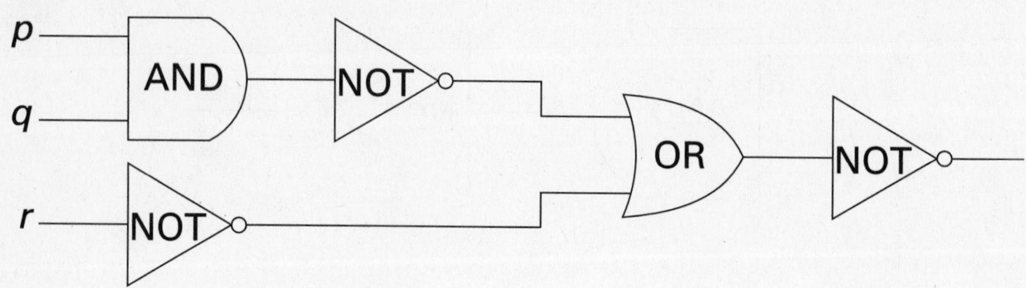

5.

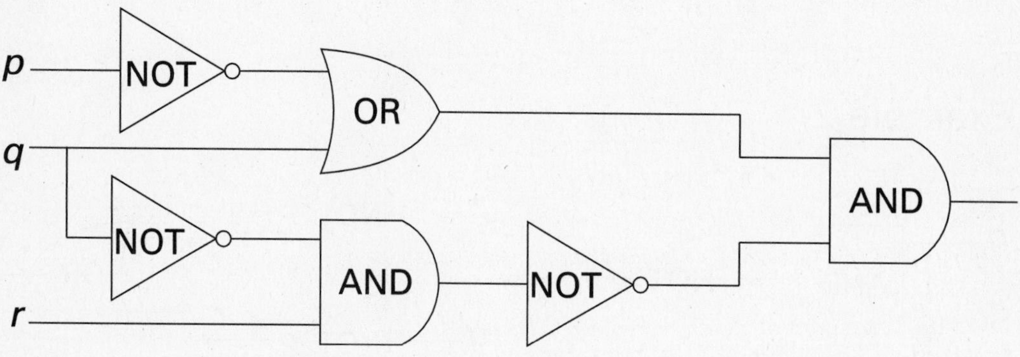

6.

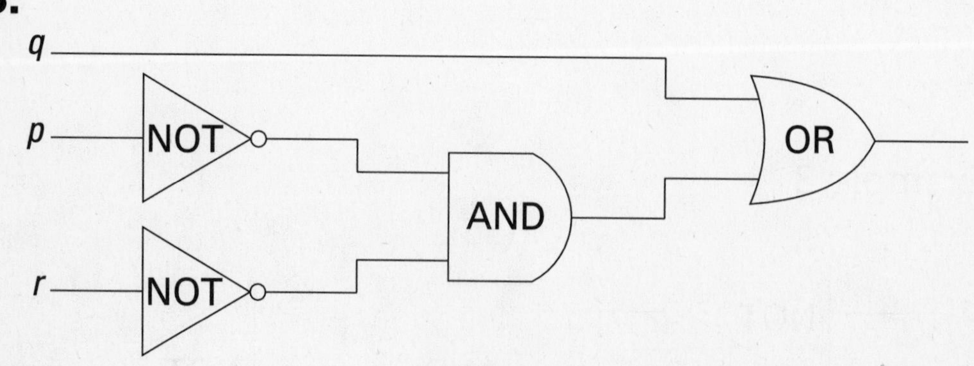

Valid Forms of Arguments

Theorem (Modus Ponens or Law of Detachment)

The following are valid forms of argument:

Simple Form	Universal Form
If p then q.	$\forall$ *x, if p(x) then q(x).*
p	*p(c), for a particular c.*
$\therefore$ *q*	$\therefore$ *q(c)*

Theorem (The Law of Transitivity)

The following are valid forms of argument:

Simple Form	Universal Form
If p then q.	$\forall$ *x, if p(x), then q(x).*
If q then r.	$\forall$ *x, if q(x), then r(x).*
$\therefore$ *If p then r.*	$\therefore$ $\forall$ *x, if p(x), then r(x).*

Theorem (Modus Tollens or Law of Indirect Reasoning)

The following are valid forms of argument:

Simple Form	Universal Form
If p then q.	$\forall$ *x, if p(x) then q(x).*
not q.	*not q(c), for a particular c.*
$\therefore$ *not p.*	$\therefore$ *not p(c) for that c.*

Warm-up

Lesson 2-1

Write the solutions to each inequality using interval notation.

1. $1 \le x \le 8$ **2.** $2 < y \le 9$ **3.** $3 \le z$

4. $w < 4$ **5.** $v > 5$

Warm-up

Lesson 2-2

Graph the function f with $f(r) = 2\pi r^2 + \frac{116}{r}$. Trace along the graph. How close can you get to the values for $f(1)$, $f(2)$, $f(3)$, and $f\left(\frac{1}{2}\right)$ given at the bottom of page 87 of the Student Edition?

Warm-up

Lesson 2-3

In 1–4, a real function f is described by an equation. Tell whether f is increasing, decreasing, or neither increasing nor decreasing on the interval [-1,1].

1. $f(x) = x^2$

2. $f(x) = x^3$

3. $f(x) = \sqrt{x}$

4. $f(x) = |x|$

5. $f(x) = \sin x$

Warm-up

Lesson 2-4

A function g is described. As x gets larger and larger, what happens to $g(x)$? Choose one of the following:

(a) $g(x)$ becomes larger and larger, ultimately larger than any number you might pick.

(b) $g(x)$ becomes larger and larger, approaching a particular value.

(c) $g(x)$ has no limit.

(d) $g(x)$ becomes smaller and smaller, ultimately smaller than any number you might pick.

(e) $g(x)$ becomes smaller and smaller, approaching a particular value.

1. $g(x) = 4 - 3x$

2. $g(x) = 2^{-x}$

3. $g(x) = 1 - 2^{-x}$

4. $g(x) = \sin(2x)$

5. $g(x) = x^{107}$

Warm-up

Lesson 2-5

Determine how to enter parametric equations on your calculator. Graph the following pairs of parametric equations for all real values of the parameter t. Describe the graph.

1. $x = t$, $y = t^2$

2. $x = t^2$, $y = t$

3. $x = 2t^2 + 4t - 6$; $y = t^2 + 2t - 3$

Warm-up
Lesson 2-6

Give the value of each expression.

1. $\cos \frac{5\pi}{6}$

2. $\sin \frac{5\pi}{6}$

3. $\cos^2\left(\frac{5\pi}{6}\right) + \sin^2\left(\frac{5\pi}{6}\right)$

4. $\tan \frac{5\pi}{6}$

Warm-up
Lesson 2-7

In 1–4, let x be any real number. Give the limit of the expression as $x \to \infty$ and as $x \to -\infty$.

1. 2^x

2. 0.9^x

3. $5 \cdot 6^x$

4. $-2 \cdot 3^x$

Warm-up
Lesson 2-8

Give an explicit formula and a recursive formula for each sequence.

1. The arithmetic sequence 2000, 2001, 2002, 2003, . . .

2. The geometric sequence 5, 4.5, 4.05, . . .

Warm-up
Lesson 2-9

In 1–4, evaluate each of the following expressions without using a calculator.

1. $\log_2 8$

2. $\log_8 2$

3. $\log 2 + \log 50$

4. $\ln \sqrt{e}$

5. Explain, without using a calculator, why log 5,000,000 is between 6 and 7.

Intervals

Intervals whose graphs are segments:

	Interval notation	Set notation
Closed intervals from *a* to *b* (endpoint included)		
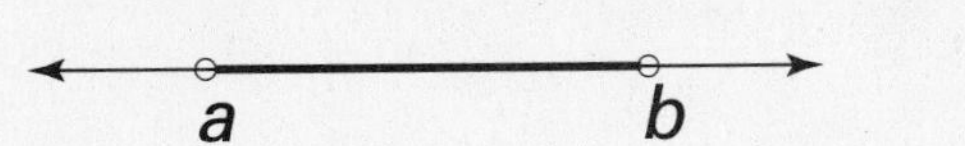	**[*a*, *b*]**	$\{x: a \leq x \leq b\}$
Open interval from *a* to *b* (endpoints not included)		
	**(*a*, *b*)**	$\{x: a < x < b\}$
Half-open interval from *a* to *b*, including *a* (one endpoint included)		
	**[*a*, *b*)**	$\{x: a \leq x < b\}$

Intervals whose graphs are rays:

Closed infinite intervals		
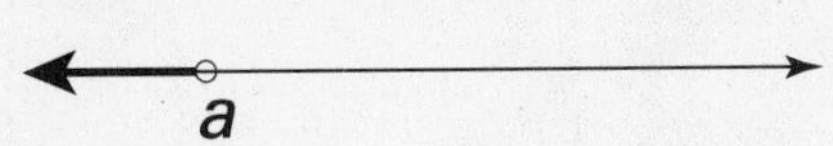	**[*b*, ∞)**	$\{x: b \leq x)$
Open infinite interval		
	(-∞, *a*)	$\{x: x < a\}$

Surface Area of a Cylinder

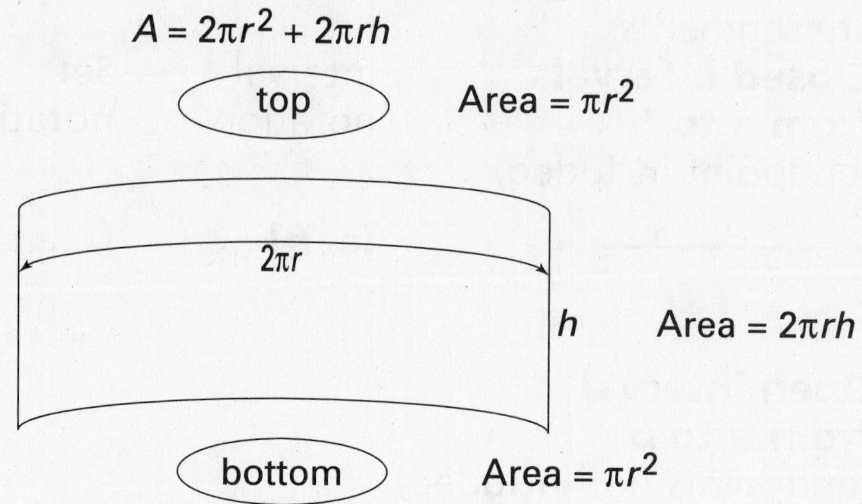

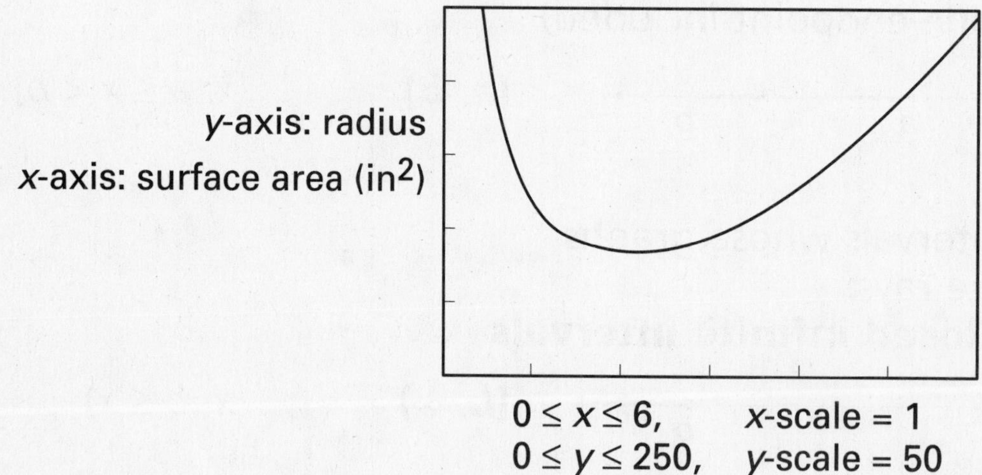

Table of Energy Consumption in the U.S.

Year	Consumption (Quadrillion BTUS)	Year	Consumption (Quadrillion BTUS)
1954	35.27	1975	70.55
1955	38.82	1976	74.36
1956	40.38	1977	76.29
1957	40.48	1978	78.09
1958	40.35	1979	78.90
1959	42.14	1980	75.96
1960	43.80	1981	73.99
1961	44.46	1982	70.85
1962	46.53	1983	70.52
1963	48.33	1984	74.14
1964	50.50	1985	73.98
1965	52.68	1986	74.30
1966	55.66	1987	76.89
1967	57.57	1988	80.22
1968	61.00	1989	81.33
1969	64.19	1990	84.17
1970	66.43	1991	84.05
1971	67.89	1992	85.26
1972	71.26	1993	87.03
1973	74.28	1994	88.90
1974	72.54	1995	90.62

Graph of Energy Consumption in the U.S.

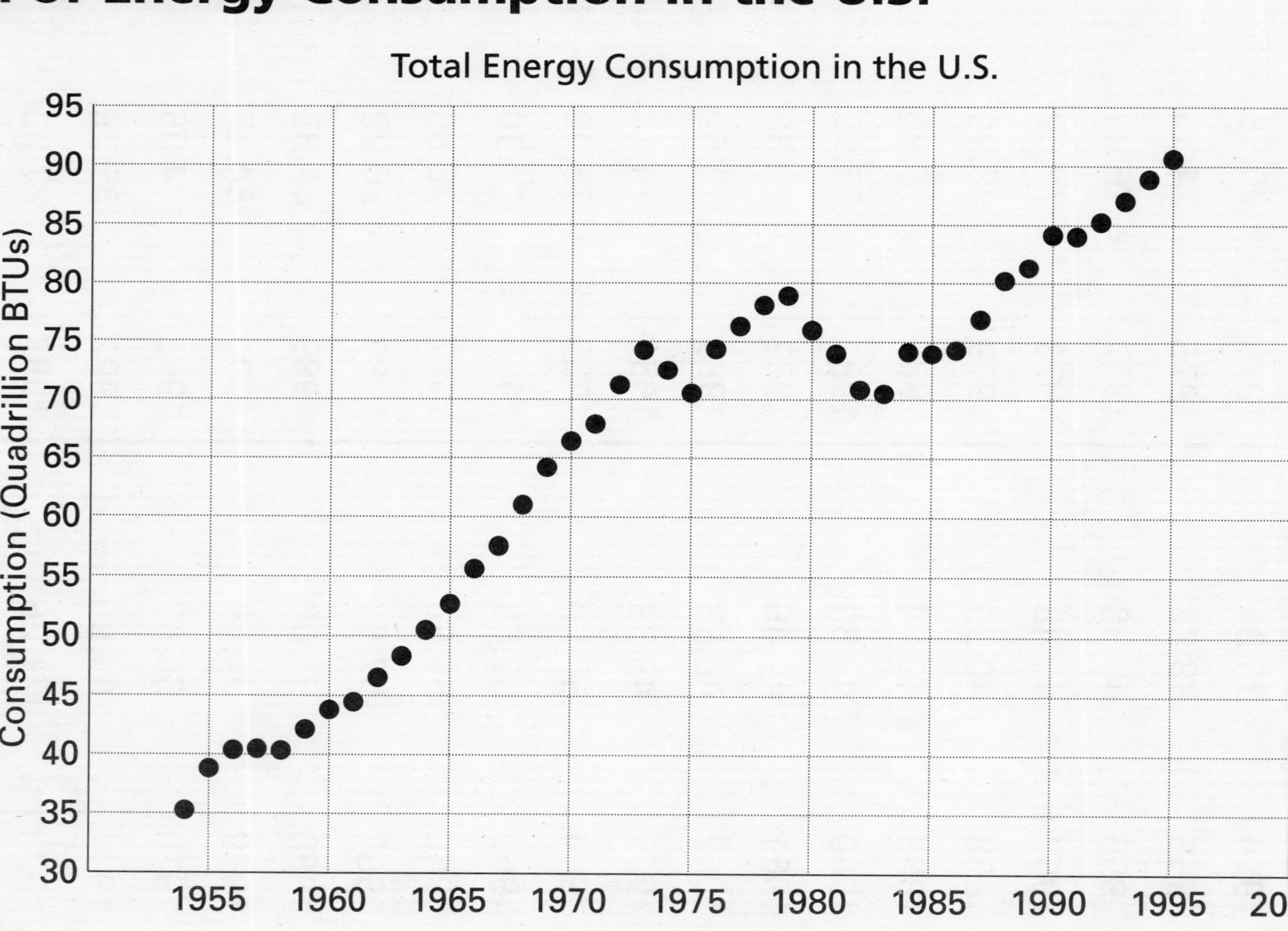

Definitions of Increasing Function and Decreasing Function

Definitions

Suppose f is a real function and S is a subset of the domain of f.

f is increasing on *S*

if and only if $\forall$ x_1 and x_2 in S, if $x_1 < x_2$ then $f(x_1) < f(x_2)$.

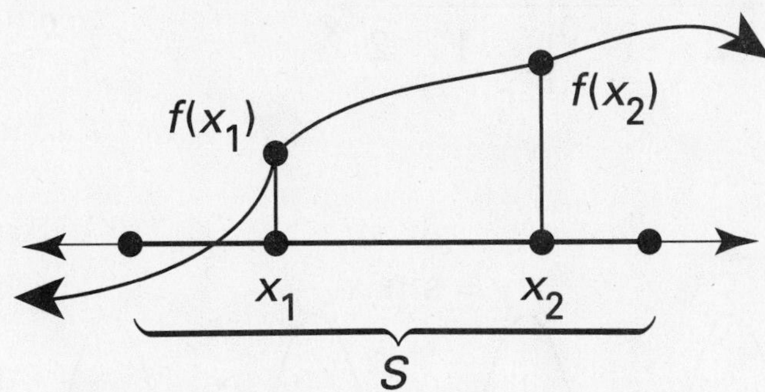

f is increasing on the interval S

f is decreasing on *S*

if and only if $\forall$ x_1 and x_2 in S, if $x_1 < x_2$ then $f(x_1) > f(x_2)$.

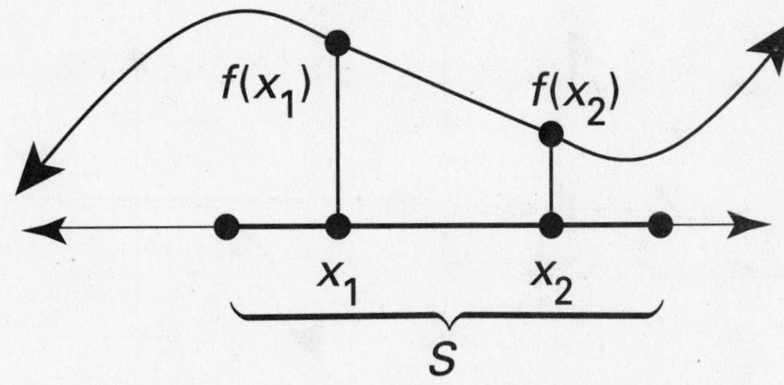

f is decreasing on the interval S

End Behavior of Exponential, Sine, and Power Functions

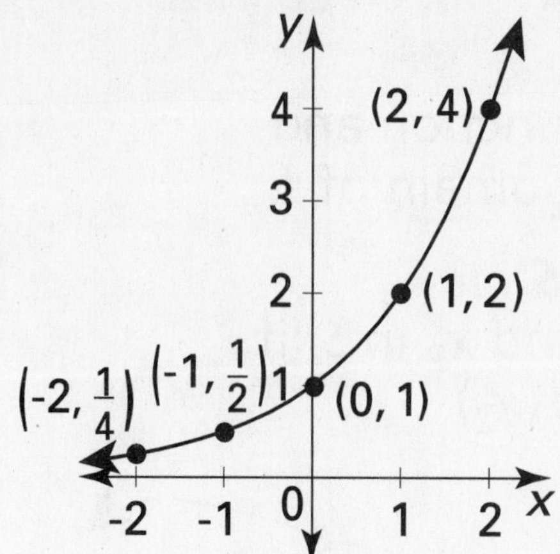

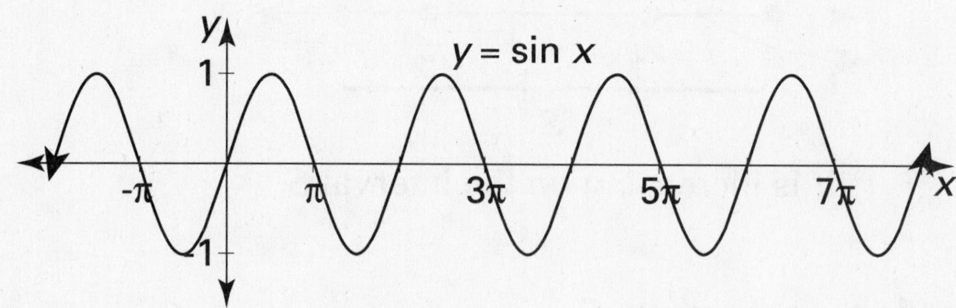

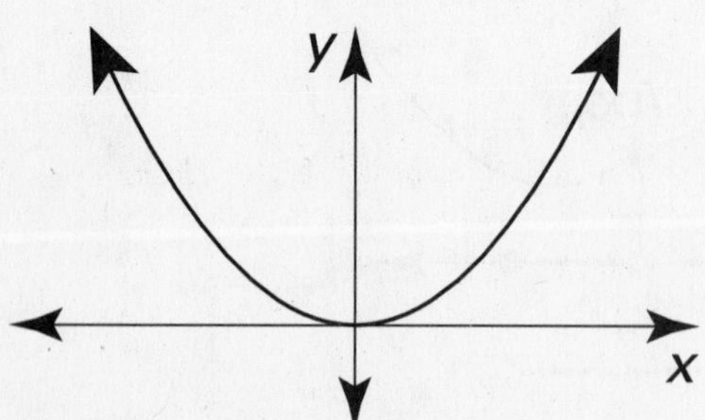

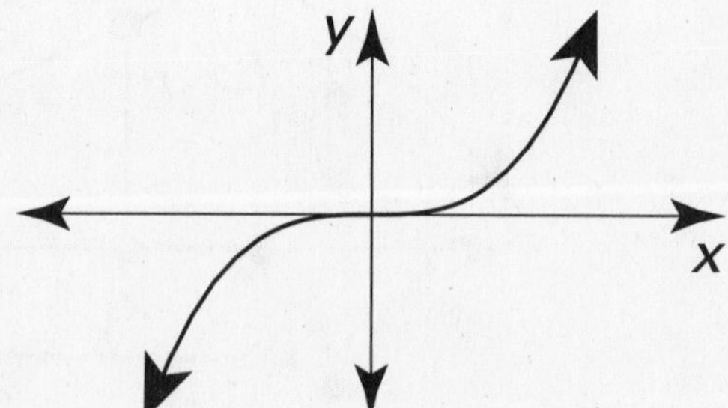

$a > 0$, n even

$\lim_{x \to \infty} ax^n = \infty$

$\lim_{x \to -\infty} ax^n = \infty$

$a > 0$, n odd

$\lim_{x \to \infty} ax^n = \infty$

$\lim_{x \to -\infty} ax^n = -\infty$

Graphs from Lesson 2-5

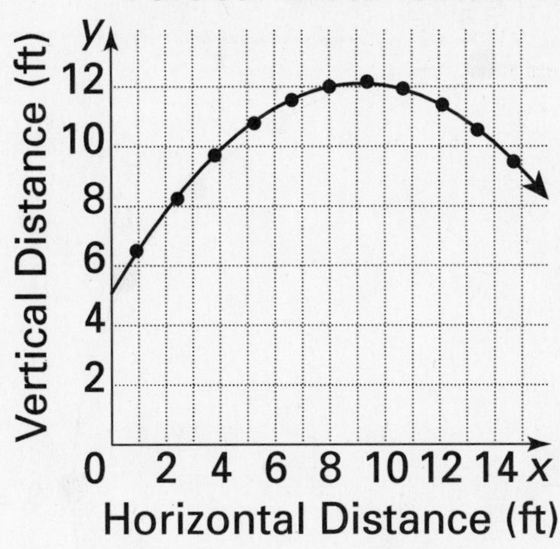

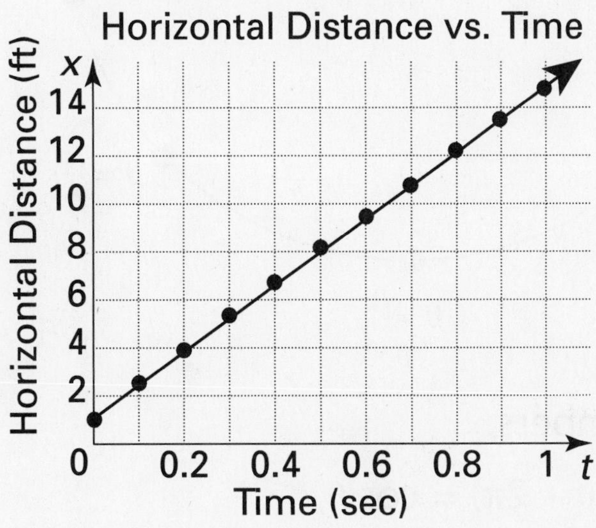

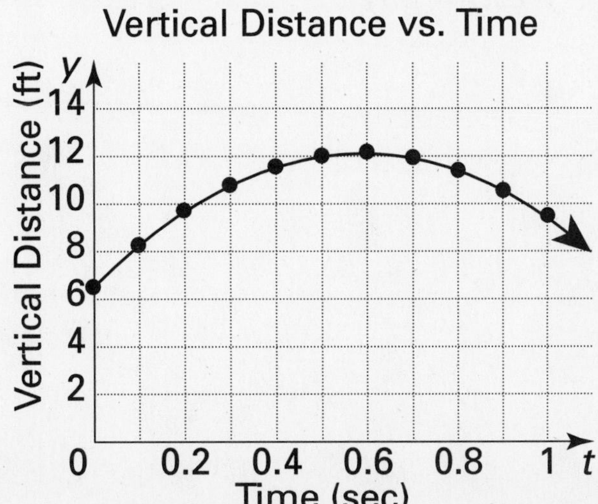

Parametric Equations for the Circle

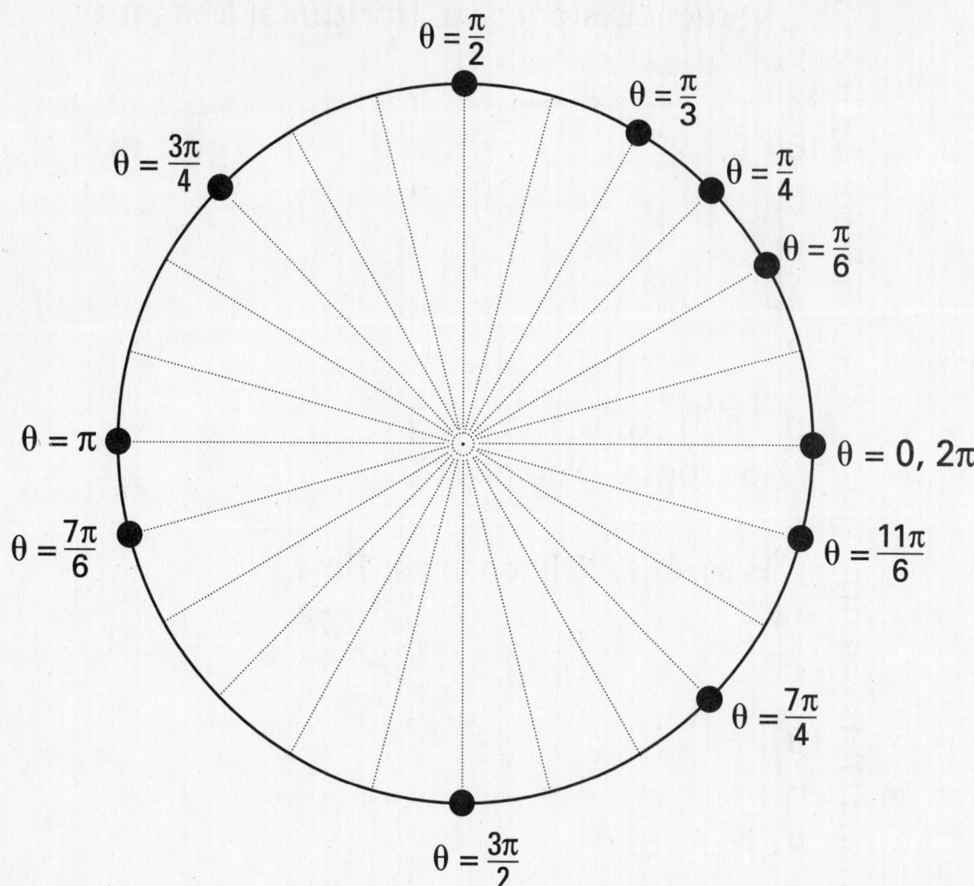

For all real numbers,

$$\cos(\theta + 2\pi) = \cos\theta,$$

$$\sin(\theta + 2\pi) = \sin\theta.$$

What is meant by "Analyzing a Function"?

1. *Domain.* Identify the values for which f is defined.

2. *Range.* Describe the set of all possible values of f.

3. *Increasing or Decreasing.* As x increases, identify the intervals on which f increases and the intervals on which f decreases.

4. *End of Behavior.* Describe what happens to f as $x \to \infty$ or as $x \to -\infty$.

5. *Maxima or Minima.* Find the greatest or least value of f.

6. *Models.* Identify situations which can be modeled by a function like f. Know how f is normally used in those situations.

7. *Properties.* Be aware of special properties of f, and their implications.

Tables from the Lesson

n	U_n
0	2000
1	2400
2	2880
3	3456
4	4147
5	4977
6	5972
7	7166
8	8600
9	10,320
10	12,383
11	14,860
12	17,832
13	21,399
14	25,678
15	30,814
16	36,977
17	44,372
18	53,247
19	63,896
20	76,675

n	U_n
0	2000
1	2373
2	2810
3	3320
4	3910
5	4591
6	5368
7	6250
8	7239
9	8338
10	9542
11	10,843
12	12,228
13	13,677
14	15,165
15	16,665
16	18,146
17	19,580
18	20,941
19	22,205
20	23,359
21	24,393
22	25,305
23	26,097
24	26,776
25	27,352
26	27,835
27	28,236

n	U_n
50	29,989
51	29,991
52	29,993
53	29,994
54	29,995
55	29,996
56	29,997

Definition and Properties of Logarithms

Definition

Let $b \neq 1$ be a positive real number. The ∀ real numbers x and y, y is the **logarithm of x to the base b,** written $y = \log_b x$, if and only if $x = b^y$.

Theorems

∀ real numbers r and s and ∀ positive real numbers b, u, and v with $b \neq 1$,

Law of Exponents	Law of Logarithms	
$b^r \cdot b^s = b^{r+s}$	$\log_b(u \cdot v) = \log_b u + \log_b v$	**Logarithm of a Product**
$\frac{b^r}{b^s} = b^{r-s}$	$\log_b \left(\frac{u}{v}\right) = \log_b u - \log_b v$	**Logarithm of a Quotient**
$(b^r)^s = b^{rs}$	$\log_b(u^s) = s \log_b u$	**Logarithm of Power**

Change of Base Theorem

Let a and b be positive real numbers both unequal to 1, then for all $x > 0$,

$$\log_b x = \log_b a \cdot \log_a x.$$

Warm-up

Lesson 3-1

Suppose that for all x, $f(x) = \sin x$ and $g(x) = \cos x$.

1. Describe the graph of h, where $h(x) = \sin x + \cos x$.
2. Describe the graph of p, where $p(x) = \frac{\sin x}{\cos x}$.

Warm-up

Lesson 3-2

Let $f(z) = 2z^3 + 4$ and $g(z) = 5z^6 + 7$.

1. Calculate $f(0)$, $g(0)$, $f \circ g(0)$, and $g \circ f(0)$.
2. Give a formula for $f \circ g(z)$, and a formula for $g \circ f(z)$.

Warm-up

Lesson 3-3

The equation $ax + b = cx + d$ is solved for x and there is exactly one solution.

1. What is the solution?
2. What must be true of a and c?

Warm-up

Lesson 3-4

Does the graph of $y = \frac{(x-2)^2}{x-2}$ ever intersect the x-axis? Explain.

Warm-up

Lesson 3-5

The sum of a positive number and its reciprocal is less than 2. What is the number?

Warm-up

Lesson 3-6

Find the zeros of the function h defined by $h(x) = (x + 3)^4 + (x + 3)^2 - 5 = 7$.

Warm-up

Lesson 3-7

Find all solutions to $(4x + 5)(\sin x - 0.5) = 0$ on the interval $[-2\pi, 2\pi]$.

Warm-up

Lesson 3-8

If the scale change S is defined as $S:(x, y) \rightarrow (4x, 5y)$ and the translation T is defined as $T:(x, y) \rightarrow (x + 1, y - 6)$, what is the image of the equation $y = x^2$ under the composite $T \circ S$?

Warm-up

Lesson 3-9

1. Graph $y = |3x - 22|$.

2. Graph $y = 2x$ on the graph from Question 1. Use this graph to solve the equation $|3x - 2| = 2x$.

3. Solve $|3x - 2| = 2x$ algebraically.

Warm-up

Lesson 3-10

Consider two segments, one with unit length and the other with length 6. Explain how to set up a 1-1 correspondence between the points of these two segments.

Graphs

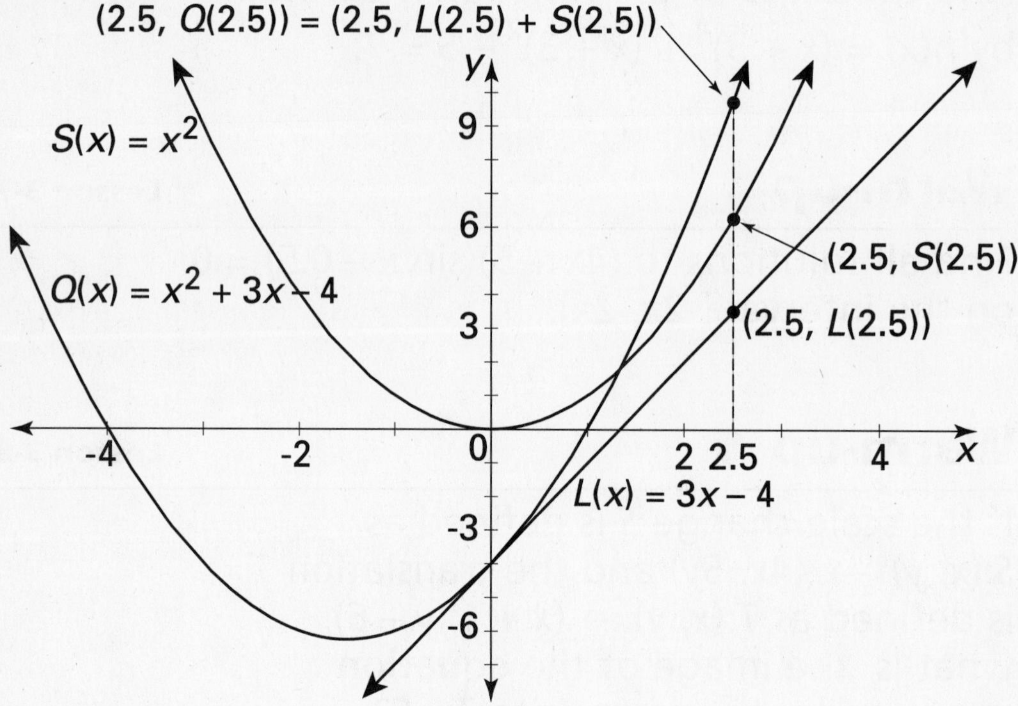
(2.5, Q(2.5)) = (2.5, L(2.5) + S(2.5))
y
9
6
3
-3
-6
S(x) = x2
Q(x) = x2 + 3x – 4
(2.5, S(2.5))
(2.5, L(2.5))
-4
-2
0
2 2.5
4
x
L(x) = 3x – 4

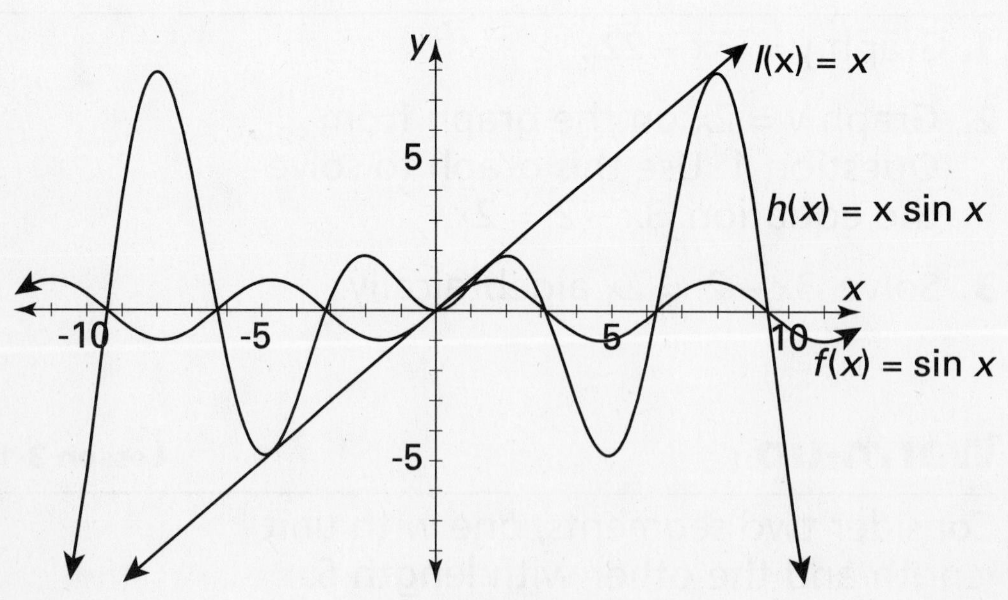
y
5
-5
I(x) = x
h(x) = x sin x
x
-10
-5
5
10
f(x) = sin x

Properties of Theorems I

Properties of Inequality and Operations

For any real expressions $f(x)$ and $g(x)$: if $f(x) < g(x)$, then

$f(x) + c < g(x) + c$	**Addition Property of Inequality**
$f(x) \cdot c < g(x) \cdot c$, if $c > 0$ $f(x) \cdot c > g(x) \cdot c$, if $c < 0$.	**Multiplication Properties of Inequality**

Theorem

Suppose that f is a real function. If f is increasing throughout its domain, or if f is decreasing throughout its domain, then f is a 1-1 function.

Corollary

If f is an increasing function throughout its domain, or if f is a decreasing function throughout its domain, then the inverse of f is a function.

Theorem

Let f be a real function.

(1) If f is increasing on its entire domain, then f^{-1} is increasing on its entire domain.

(2) If f is decreasing on its entire domain, then f^{-1} is decreasing on its entire domain.

Properties of Theorems II

Function Composition and Inequality Property (1)

For any real expressions $f(x)$, $g(x)$, and an increasing real function h:
$f(x) < g(x) \Leftrightarrow h(f(x)) < h(g(x))$.

Function Composition and Inequality Property (2)

For any real expressions $f(x)$, $g(x)$, and a decreasing real function h:
$f(x) < g(x) \Leftrightarrow h(f(x)) > h(g(x))$.

Reversible Steps Theorems for Inequalities

Let $f(x)$ and $g(x)$ be any real expressions. Then for all real expressions c and real function h:

(1) $f(x) < g(x) \Leftrightarrow f(x) + c < g(x) + c$.

(2) $f(x) < g(x) \Leftrightarrow f(x) \cdot c < g(x) \cdot c$, if $c > 0$.
$f(x) < g(x) \Leftrightarrow f(x) \cdot c > g(x) \cdot c$, if $c < 0$.

(3) $f(x) < g(x) \Leftrightarrow h(f(x)) < h(g(x))$, if h is increasing.
$f(x) < g(x) \Leftrightarrow h(f(x)) > h(g(x))$, if h is decreasing.

Circles and Ellipse

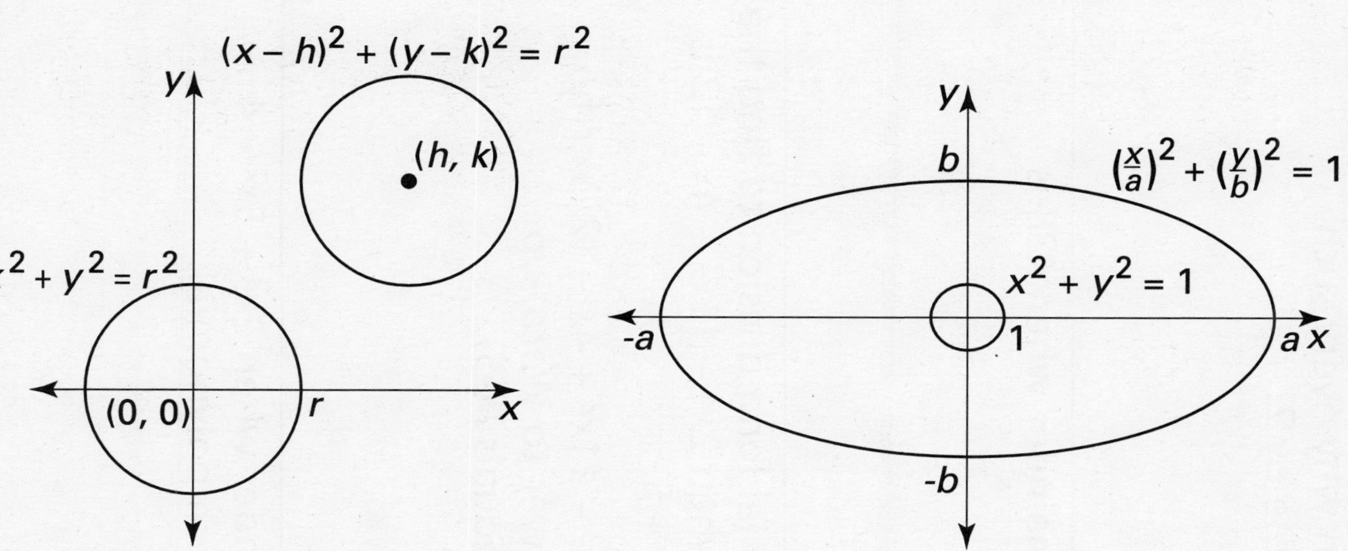

Warm-up

Lesson 4-1

Consider those six-digit integers of the form a b c a b c. (One such integer is 497497.) Explain why every such integer is divisible by 7.

Warm-up

Lesson 4-2

What is the remainder when 438 is divided by 27?

Warm-up

Lesson 4-3

1. Use polynomial long division to find the remainder when $2x^3 - 11x^2 + 4x - 12$ is divided by $x + 5$.
2. Let $P(x) = 2x^3 - 11x^2 + 4x - 12$. Verify that the answer to *Warm-up* Question 1 equals $P(-5)$.

Warm-up

Lesson 4-4

Find the remainder when $2x^3 + 5x^2 - 4$ is divided by each polynomial.

1. $x - 2$
2. $x + 4$
3. $x + 2$
4. Are any of the divisors in 1–3 factors of the given polynomial? If so which divisors.

Warm-up

Lesson 4-5

Find a number whose remainder when divided by 7 is 6. Find a number whose remainder when divided by 7 is 3. Multiply these numbers together. What is the remainder when their product is divided by 7? Share your results with a classmate. Must you get the same answer?

Warm-up

Lesson 4-6

A number has hundreds digit *h*, tens digit *t*, and units digit *u*.

1. What is the value of the number?
2. What is the value of the number formed by reversing the digits.
3. Show that the difference of the number and the number formed by reversing the digits is divisible by 11.

Warm-up

Lesson 4-7

1. How many digits does $2^{1,000,000} - 1$ have in base 10?
2. Explain why $2^{1,000,000} - 1$ is not a prime number.

Definitions and Basic Theorems of Divisibility I

Definition

Suppose that n and d are integers and $d \neq 0$. ***d* is a factor of *n*** if and only if there is an integer q such that $n = q \cdot d$.

Definition

Suppose that $n(x)$ and $d(x)$ are polynomials and d is not the zero function. ***d*(*x*) is a factor of *n*(*x*)** if and only if there exists a polynomial $q(x)$ such that $n(x) = q(x) \cdot d(x)$.

Theorem (Transitive Property of Integer Function)

For all integers a, b, and c, if a is a factor of b and b is a factor of c, then a is a factor of c.

Theorem (Factor of an Integer Sum)

For all integers a, b, and c, if a is a factor of b and a is a factor of c, then a is a factor of $b + c$.

Definitions and Basic Theorems of Divisibility II

Theorems

For all polynomials $a(x)$, $b(x)$, and $c(x)$:

Transitive Property of Polynomial Factors

If $a(x)$ is a factor of $b(x)$ and $b(x)$ is a factor of $c(x)$, then $a(x)$ is a factor of $c(x)$.

Factor of a Polynomial Sum Theorem

If $a(x)$ is a factor of $b(x)$ and $a(x)$ is a factor of $c(x)$, then $a(x)$ is a factor of $b(x) + c(x)$.

Theorem (Factor of an Integer Product)

For all integers m, n, and p, if m is a factor of n, then m is a factor of $n \bullet p$.

Long Division of Polynomials

$$
\begin{array}{r}
3x^2 - 6x + 7 \\
2x + 1 \overline{\big) 6x^3 - 9x^2 + 8x + 1} \\
\underline{6x^3 + 3x^2 } \\
-12x^2 + 8x + 1 \\
\underline{-12x^2 - 6x } \\
14x + 1 \\
\underline{14x + 7} \\
-6
\end{array}
$$

$$
\begin{array}{r}
3x^3 - 2x^2 + x - \frac{1}{2} \\
2x^2 + x \overline{\big) 6x^5 - x^4 + 0x^3 + 0x^2 + x + 1} \\
\underline{6x^5 + 3x^4 } \\
-4x^4 + 0x^3 + 0x^2 + x + 1 \\
\underline{-4x^4 - 2x^3 } \\
2x^3 + 0x^2 + x + 1 \\
\underline{2x^3 + x^2 } \\
-x^2 + x + 1 \\
\underline{-x^2 - \frac{1}{2}x } \\
\frac{3}{2}x + 1
\end{array}
$$

Long Division and the Quotient-Remainder Theorem

$$\begin{array}{r} 485 \\ 9\overline{)4369} \\ \underline{3600} \\ 769 \\ \underline{720} \\ 49 \\ \underline{45} \\ 4 \end{array}$$

Quotient-Remainder Theorem Version

$$4369 = 9 \cdot 400 + 769$$

$$769 = 9 \cdot 80 + 49$$

$$49 = 9 \cdot 5 + 4$$

$$\therefore \quad 4369 = 9 \cdot 400 + 9 \cdot 80 + 9 \cdot 5 + 4$$

$$\begin{array}{r} 3x^2 - 6x + 7 \\ 2x + 1\overline{)6x^3 - 9x^2 + 8x + 1} \\ \underline{6x^3 + 3x^2 \qquad\qquad} \\ -12x^2 + 8x + 1 \\ \underline{-12x^2 - 6x \qquad} \\ 14x + 1 \\ \underline{14x + 7} \\ -6 \end{array}$$

Quotient-Remainder Theorem Version

$$6x^3 - 9x^2 + 8x + 1 = (2x + 1) \cdot 3x^2 + (-12x^2 + 8x + 1)$$

$$-12x^2 + 8x + 1 = (2x + 1) \cdot (-6x) + (14x + 1)$$

$$14x + 1 = (2x + 1) \cdot 7 + (-6)$$

$$\therefore \quad 6x^3 - 9x^2 + 8x + 1 = (2x + 1) \cdot 3x^2 + (2x + 1)(-6x) + (2x + 1) \cdot 7 + (-6)$$

$$= (2x + 1)(3x^2 - 6x + 7) + (-6)$$

Question 8

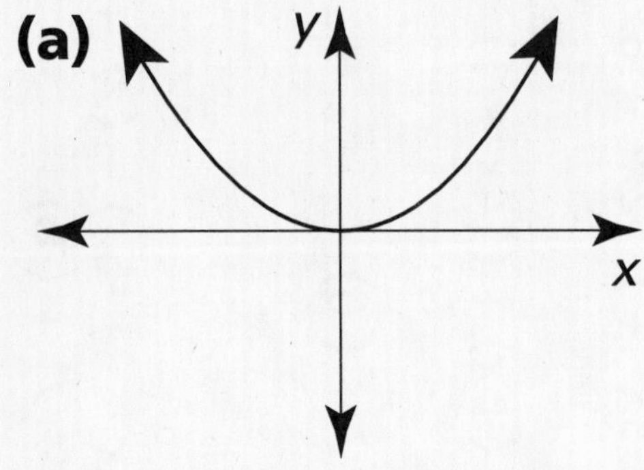

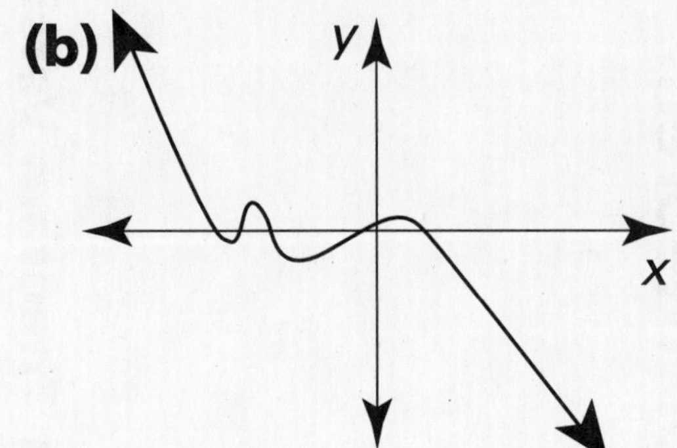

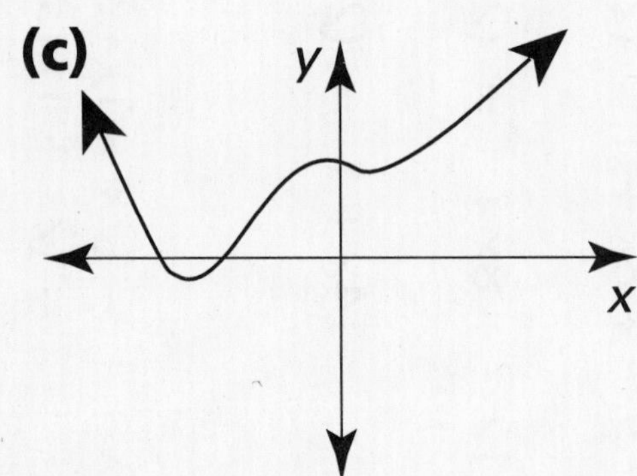

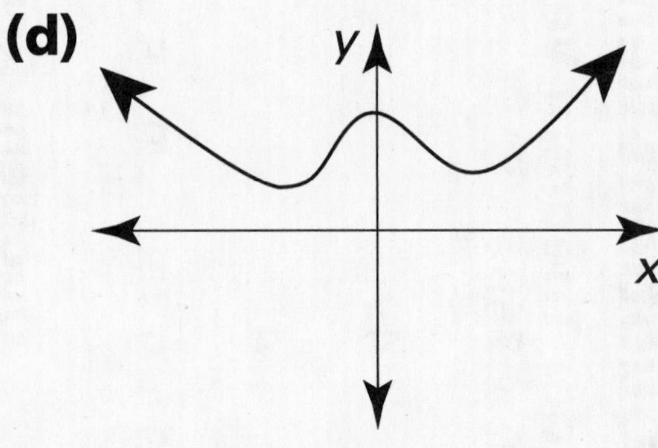

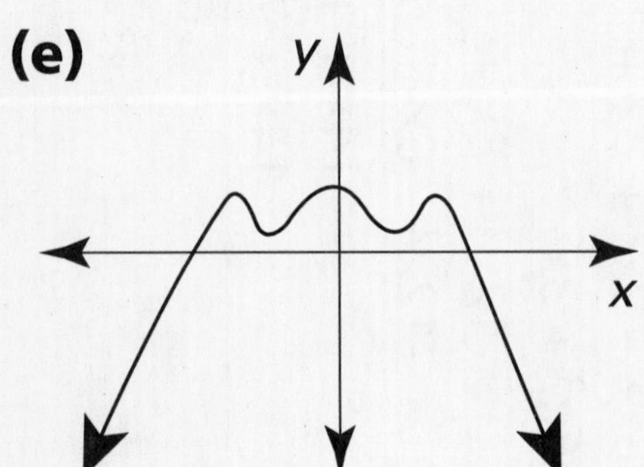

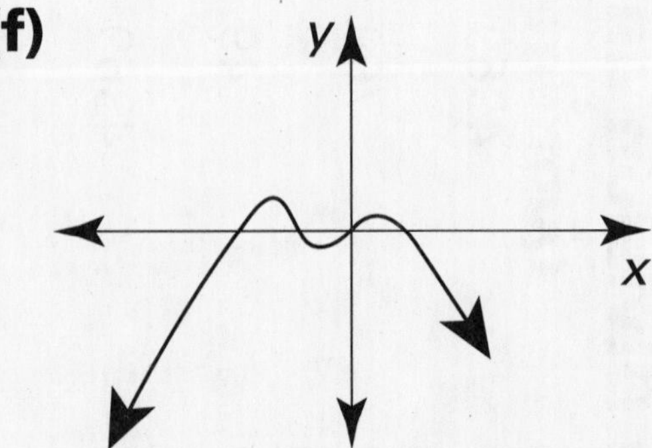

Integers in Base 10 and Base 2

Base 10 Integer	Base 2 Place Values 2^4 16	2^3 8	2^2 4	2^1 2	2^0 1	Base 2 Integer
0	0	0	0	0	0	0_2
1	0	0	0	0	1	1_2
2	0	0	0	1	0	10_2
3	0	0	0	1	1	11_2
4	0	0	1	0	0	100_2
5	0	0	1	0	1	101_2
6	0	0	1	1	0	110_2
7	0	0	1	1	1	111_2
8	0	1	0	0	0	1000_2
9	0	1	0	0	1	1001_2
10	0	1	0	1	0	1010_2
11	0	1	0	1	1	1011_2
12	0	1	1	0	0	1100_2
13	0	1	1	0	1	1101_2
14	0	1	1	1	0	1110_2
15	0	1	1	1	1	1111_2
16	1	0	0	0	0	10000_2

Half-Adder Network

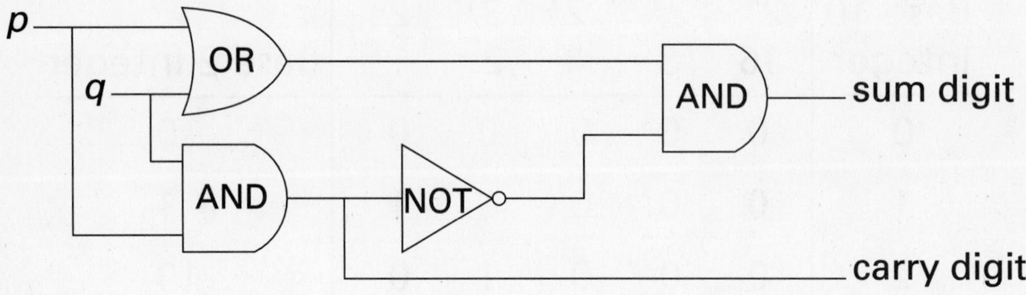

p	q	sum digit	carry digit
1	1	0	1
1	0	1	0
0	1	1	0
0	0	0	0

Definitions and Theorems I

Definition

An integer $n > 1$ is **prime** if and only if 1 and n are the only positive integer factors of n.

Prime Factor Theorem

Every integer greater than 1 is either prime or has a prime factor.

Theorem (Validity of Proof by Contradiction)

The following form of argument is valid.

If not *s* then (*p* and (not *p*)).
$\therefore$ *s*.

Infinitude of Primes Theorem

There are infinitely many prime numbers.

Factor Search Theorem

If an integer n has no prime factors between 1 and $\sqrt{n}$ inclusive, then n is prime.

Definitions and Theorems II

Fundamental Theorem of Arithmetic

Suppose that n is an integer and that $n > 1$. Then either n is a prime number or n has a prime factorization which is unique except for the order of the factors.

Definition

A polynomial $p(x)$ with degree $n \geq 1$ is **prime over the real numbers** if and only if the only polynomial factors of $p(x)$ with real coefficients and leading coefficient 1 are constants or constant multiples of $p(x)$.

Unique Factorization Theorem for Polynomials

Suppose that $p(x)$ is a polynomial with integer coefficients. Then either $p(x)$ is prime over the real numbers or $p(x)$ has a factorization into polynomials prime over the reals which is unique except for the order of the factors or multiplications by real constants.

Warm-up

Lesson 5-1

When it is m minutes after 5:00 and not yet 5:30, the minute hand on a clock will have rotated $6m$ degrees clockwise from straight up, and the hour hand will have rotated $\frac{m}{2}$ degrees clockwise from the 5:00 position.

1. What is the origin of the fraction $\frac{m}{2}$?
2. What is the measure of the angle between the hour hand and the minute hand? Write this measure as a single fraction.
3. At what time will the minute hand cross the hour hand?

Warm-up

Lesson 5-2

Write the sum $\frac{a}{b} + \frac{c}{d} - \frac{e}{f}$ as a single fraction, and check your answer.

Warm-up

Lesson 5-3

Compare the graphs of $y = \frac{1}{x^2}$ and $y = \frac{1}{x^4}$. Name two ways in which they are alike, and tell how they are different.

Warm-up

Lesson 5-4

You fill up your car's gas tank with 14.3 gallons of gas when its odometer shows 12345.6 miles, and you fill it up again with 13.7 gallons when its odometer shows 12698.4 miles. How many miles per gallon is your car getting?

Warm-up

Lesson 5-5

Give an equation for a function f such that $\lim\limits_{x \to \infty} f(x) = 6$.

Warm-up

Lesson 5-6

1. Find a recursive formula for the first four terms of the sequence $\frac{3}{2}, \frac{7}{5}, \frac{17}{12}, \frac{41}{29}, \frac{99}{70}, \ldots$
2. Use your formula to obtain the next few terms of the sequence. Does the sequence seem to have a limit? If so, conjecture what that limit is?

Warm-up

Lesson 5-7

In right triangle *ABC*, there are six possible ratios of sides.

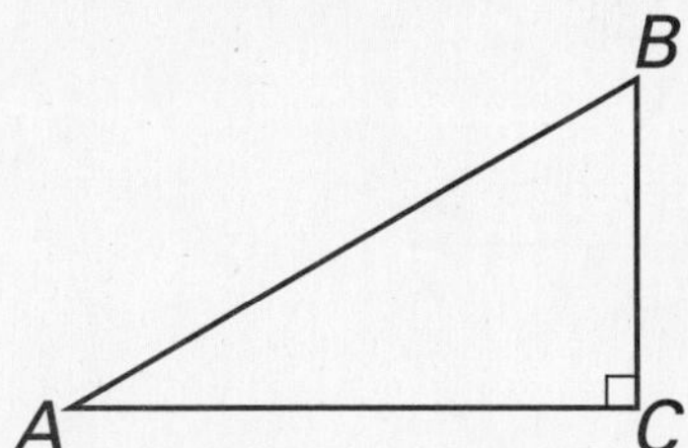

1. Write these six ratios.

2. Match these ratios with the following six numbers: sin *A*, cos *A*, tan *A*, cot *A*, sec *A*, and csc *A*.

Warm-up

Lesson 5-8

A trucker drives 25 miles from city A to city B in 40 minutes. The trucker wants to drive the 20 miles from city B to city C so as to average 55 mph for the entire trip. Is this possible? At what average speed must the trucker travel from city B to city C?

Warm-up

Lesson 5-9

Define each term.

1. Unit fraction

2. Regular polygon

3. Regular polyhedron

Graph of $f(x) = \frac{1}{x}$

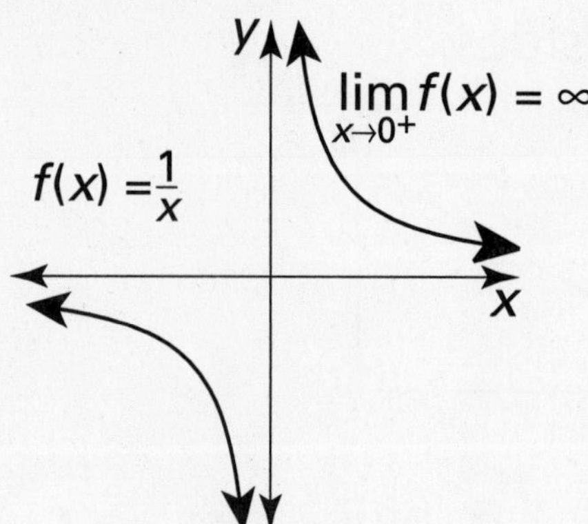

Additional Examples

1. Consider the function f with rule $f(x) = \frac{1}{x-3} + 2$, where $x \neq 3$, graphed here.

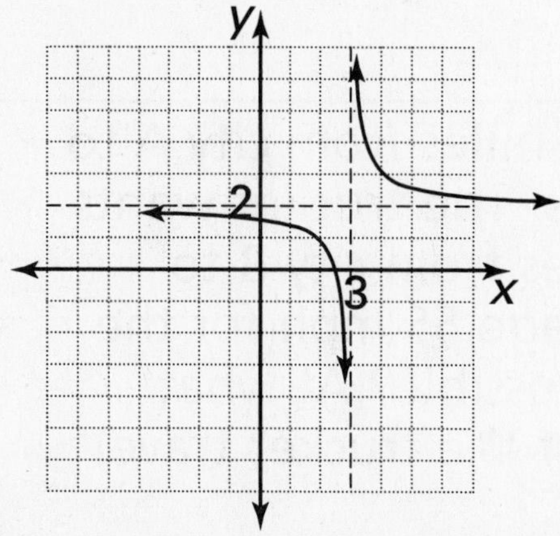

a. Give an equation for the vertical asymptote to the graph.

b. Use limit notation to describe the behavior of the function near this asymptote.

2. a. Describe the behavior of the function $g: x \to \frac{5}{x^4}$ as x approaches 0.

b. Graph g.

Graph of $S(x) = \frac{10}{x(x + 10)}$

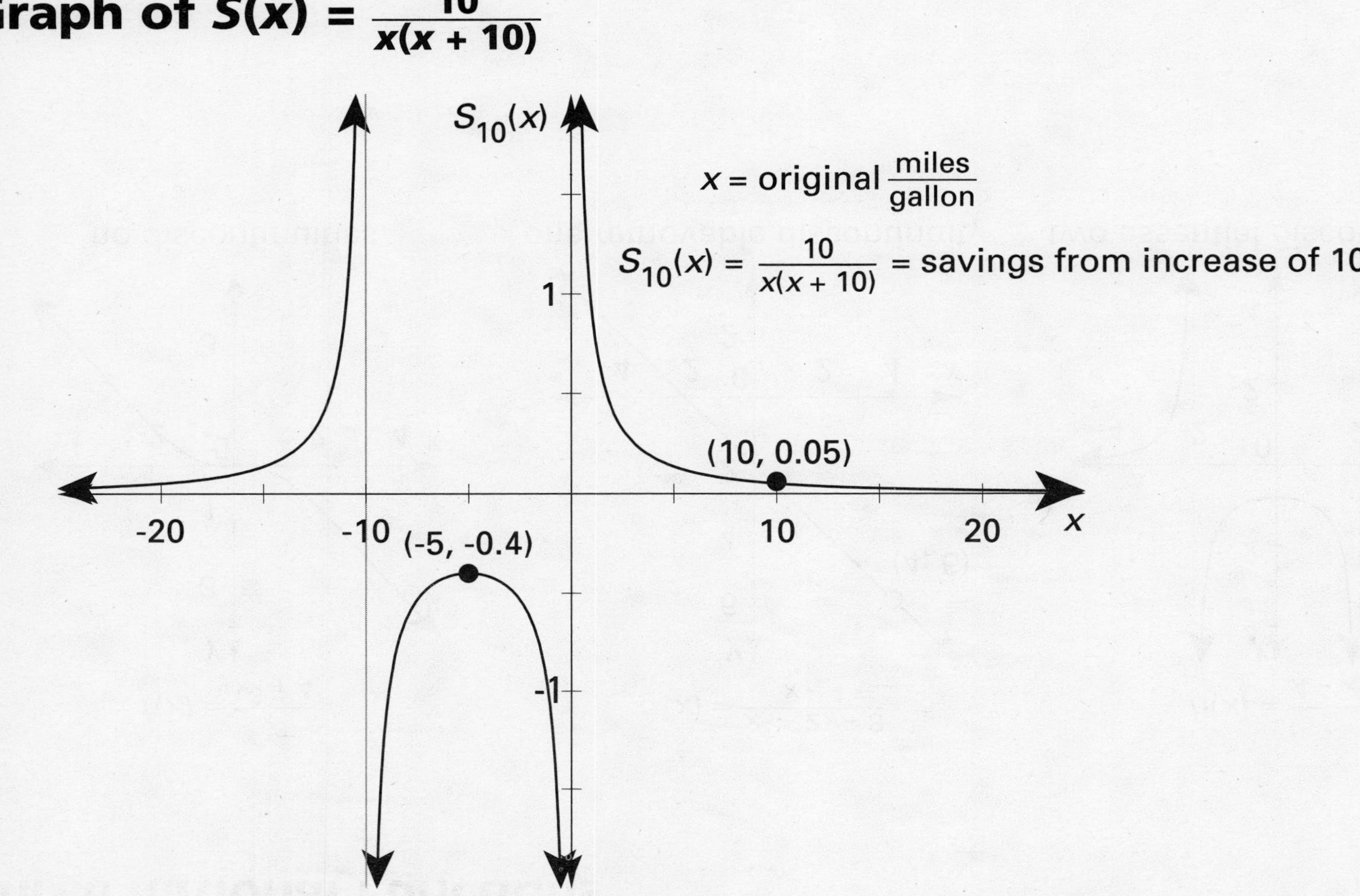

Three Rational Functions

$f(x) = \dfrac{x^3}{x^3 + 4}$

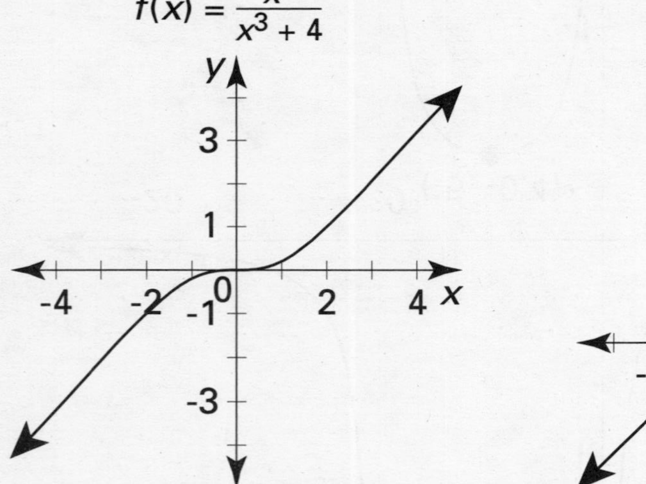

no discontinuities

$g(x) = \dfrac{x^2 - 2x - 8}{x - 4}$

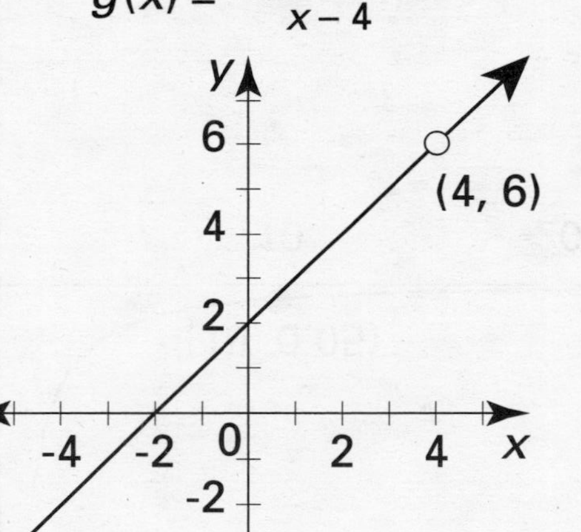

one removable discontinuity

$h(x) = \dfrac{3}{4 - x^2}$

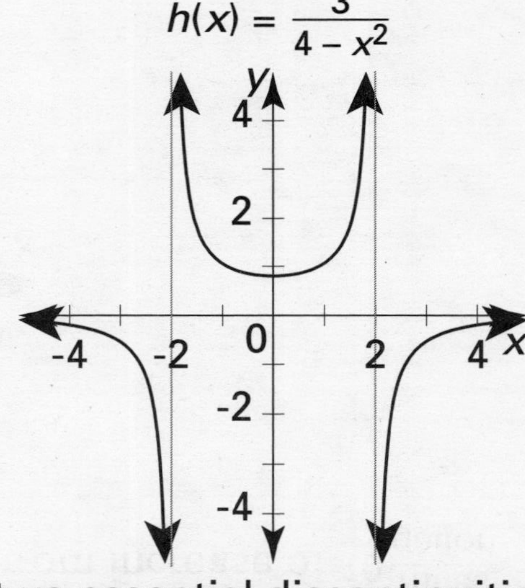

two essential discontinuities

End Behavior of Rational Functions

function rule	*m*	*n*	type	end behavior
$p(x) = 3x^4 - 5x^3 + 8x^2 - 20x + 16$	4	0	$m > n$	like the power function $f(x) = 3x^4$
$h(x) = \frac{x^2 + 14x + 12}{3x + 6}$	2	1	$m > n$ $m = n + 1$	like the linear function $f(x) = \frac{1}{3}x$
$g(x) = \frac{2x^2 + 1}{x^2 - 1}$	2	2	$m = n$	like the constant function $f(x) = 2$
$w(h) = 70\left(\frac{6400}{6400 + h}\right)^2$	0	2	$m < n$	like the reciprocal of a power function $f(h) = \frac{70 \bullet 6400^2}{h^2}$

Graphs of Sine, Cosine, and Tangent Functions

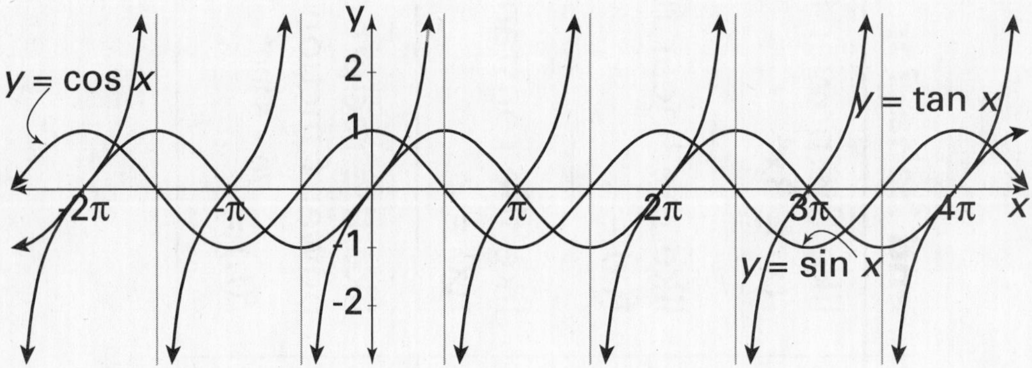

Graphs of Tangent and Cotangent Functions

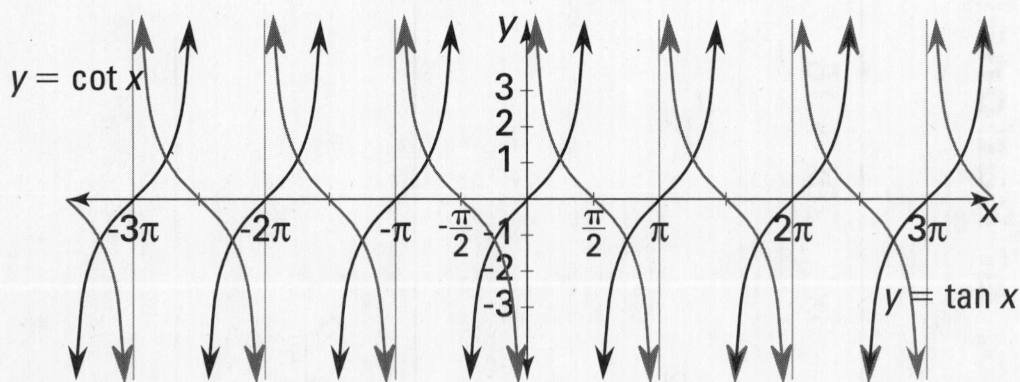

Graphs of Sine and Cosecant Functions

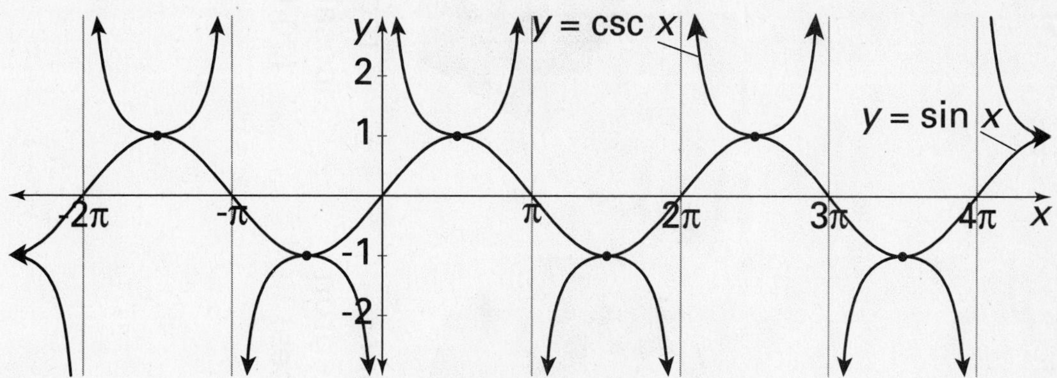

Graphs of Cosine and Secant Functions

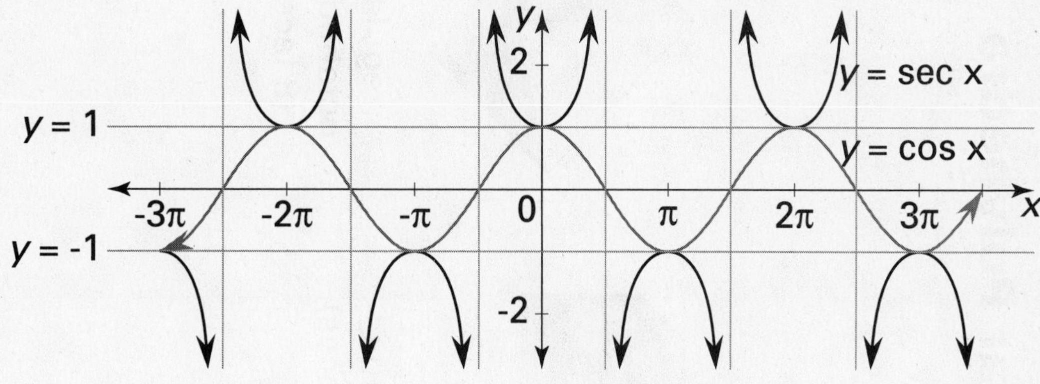

The Five Regular Polyhedra

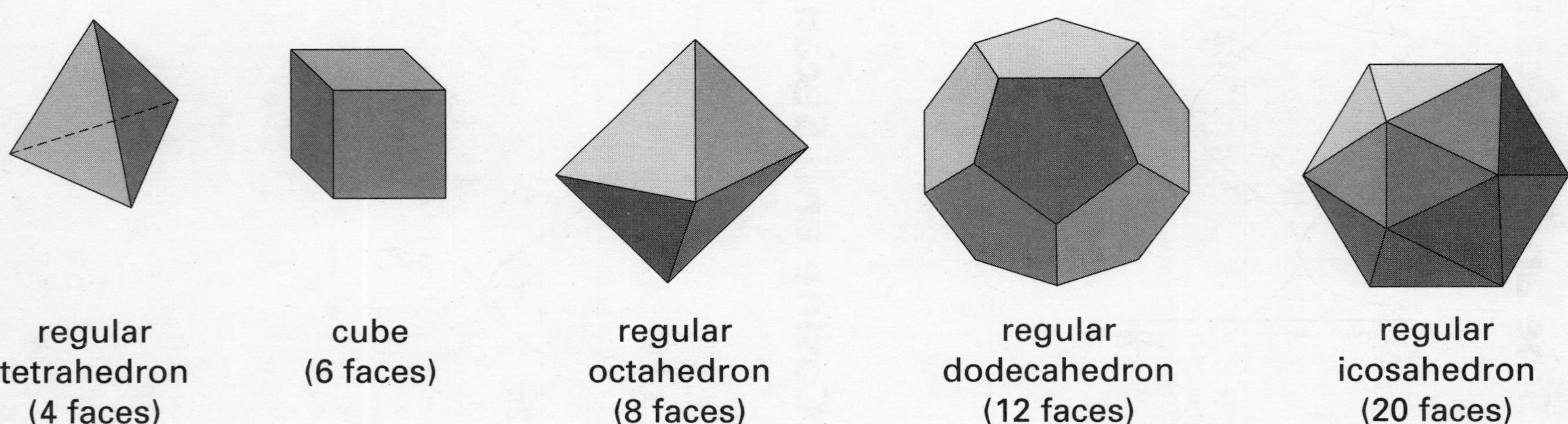

Warm-up

Lesson 6-1

1. Find a value of x for which $\sin x = \cos x$.

2. Find a value of x for which $\sin x \neq \cos x$.

3. Find a value of x for which $(\sin x)^2 + (\cos x)^2 = 1$.

Warm-up

Lesson 6-2

1. On the interval $[-2\pi, 2\pi]$ and on the same axes, graph each equation.

   a. $y = \sin x$.

   b. $y = \dfrac{2 \sin^3 x + \sin 2x \cos x}{4 \sin^2 x + 2 \cos 2x} + 0.1$

2. What identity is suggested by the result of Question 1?

Warm-up

Lesson 6-3

Consider the following table of highest and lowest temperatures (in °F) on record for each month of the year, for the city of Pittsburgh.

Month	Month Number	Highest	Lowest
January	1	69	-22
February	2	68	-12
March	3	82	-1
April	4	89	14
May	5	91	26
June	6	98	34
July	7	103	42
August	8	100	39
September	9	97	31
October	10	87	16
November	11	82	-1
December	12	74	-12

(Source: Statistical Abstract of the United States 1997)

1. a. Graph the set of ordered pairs (number of month, highest). The pattern will repeat from year to year.

b. Does it look sinusoidal?

2. a. Graph the set of ordered pairs (number of month, lowest). The pattern will repeat from year to year.

b. Does it look sinusoidal?

3. a. Graph the set of ordered pairs (highest, lowest) and place the number of the month by each point.

b. Describe the result.

Warm-up

Lesson 6-4

1. Find the distance between (cos 150°, sin 150°) and (cos 120°, sin 120°).

2. Find the distance between (cos 30°, sin 30°) and (1, 0°).

3. Generalize the results of Questions 1 and 2.

Warm-up

Lesson 6-5

If $x = \frac{\pi}{2}$ and $y = \frac{\pi}{3}$, find sin $(x + y)$, sin $(x - y)$, tan$(x + y)$, and tan $(x - y)$.

Warm-up

Lesson 6-6

Without using a calculator, find cos $2t$ and sin $2t$ for the given value of t. (These answers can be used to verify the identities for cos $2x$ and sin $2x$ found in the lesson.)

1. $t = \frac{\pi}{8}$

2. $t = -7\pi$

3. $t = -60°$

Warm-up

Lesson 6-7

Find at least one value of q that satisfies each equation.

1. $\sin q = -1$
2. $\cos q = \frac{\sqrt{3}}{2}$
3. $\tan q = -\sqrt{3}$

Warm-up

Lesson 6-8

Find all real solutions to each equation.

1. $x^2 = 1$
2. $x^3 = 1$
3. $x^4 = 1$
4. $\sqrt{x} = 1$
5. $e^x = 1$
6. $\log x = 1$
7. $\ln x = 1$
8. $|x| = 1$
9. $\lfloor x \rfloor = 1$
10. $\tan x = 1$

Questions 9-12

9. $y = \sin^2 x + \cos^2 x$

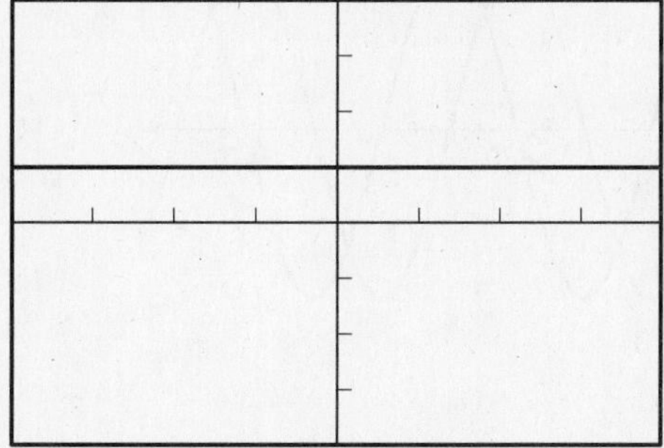

10. $y = \csc x \tan x \sin x$

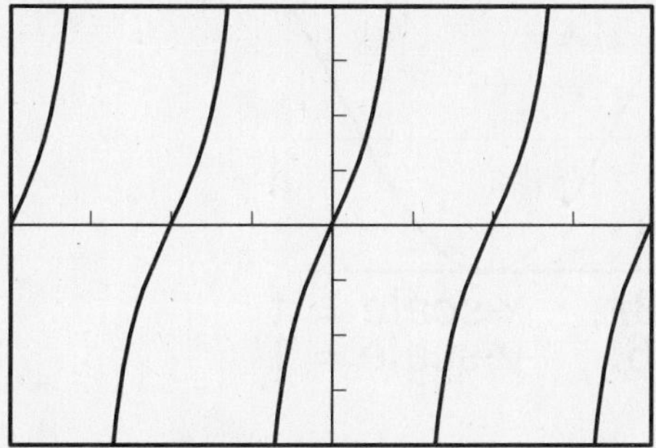

11. $y = \tan x \csc x$

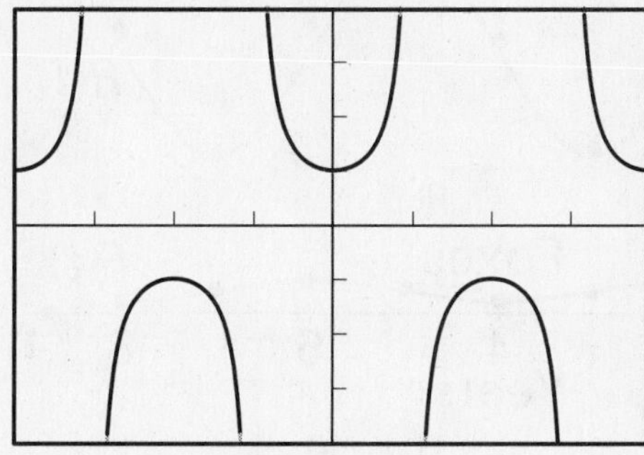

12. $y = \cos\left(\frac{3\pi}{2} + x\right)$

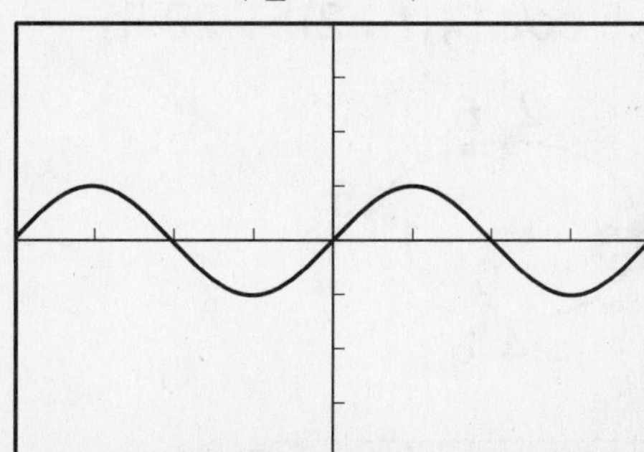

Graphs from the Lesson

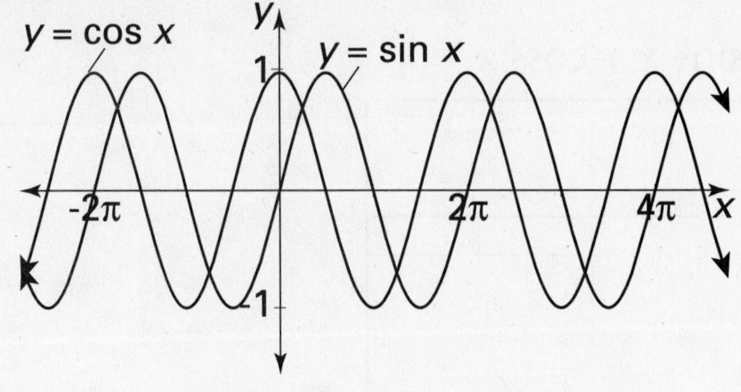

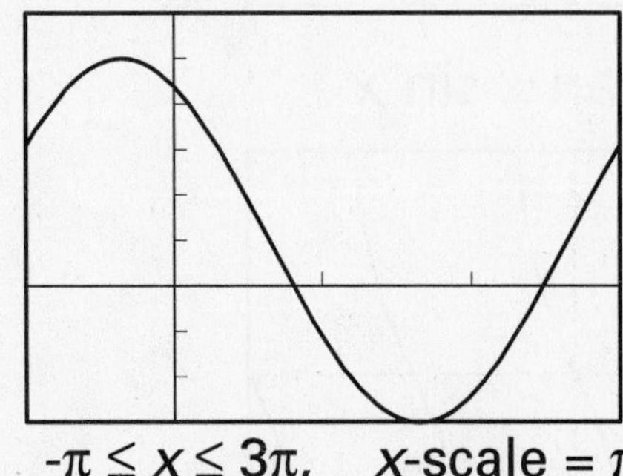

$-\pi \le x \le 3\pi$, x-scale = π
$-3 \le y \le 6$, y-scale = 1

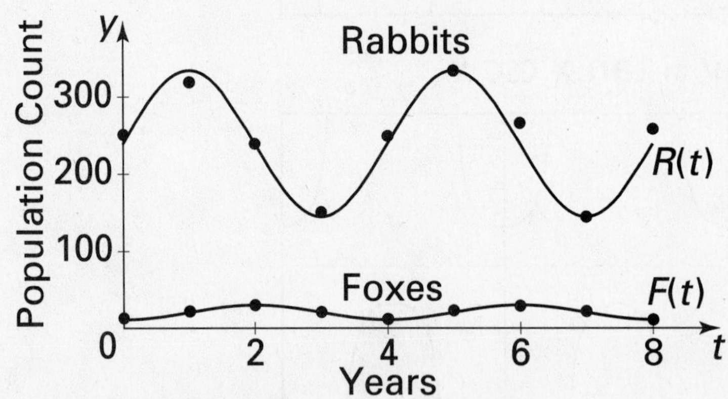

$R(t) = 95 \sin\left(\frac{\pi}{2}t\right) + 240$

$F(t) = 9.5 \cos\left(\frac{\pi}{2}(t-2)\right) + 20.5$

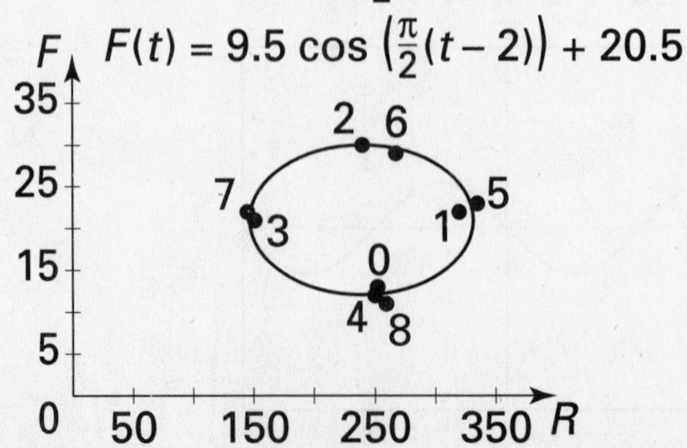

Diagram for Proof of Cosine of a Sum Theorem

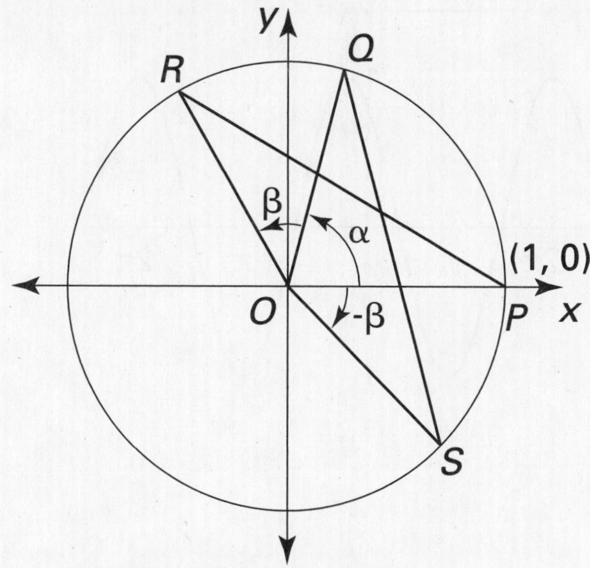

$Q = (\cos \alpha, \sin \alpha)$
$R = (\cos (\alpha + \beta), \sin (\alpha + \beta))$
$S = (\cos (-\beta), \sin (-\beta))$

Example 3 for Lesson 6-6

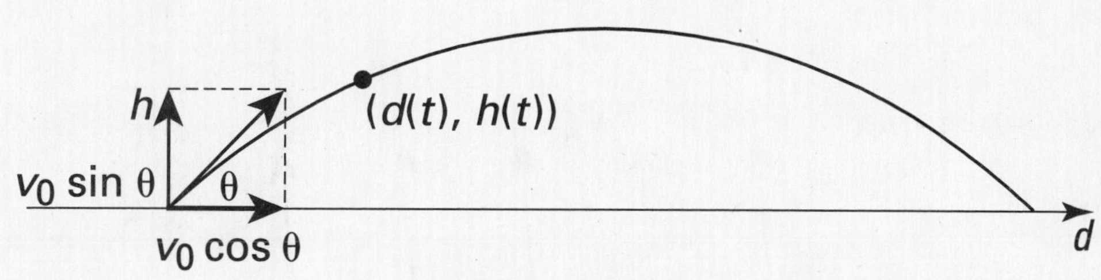

$d(t) = (v_0 \cos \theta)t$
$h(t) = -16t^2 + (v_0 \sin \theta)t$

Graphs of the Sine, Cosine, and Tangent Functions

$y = \cos x$

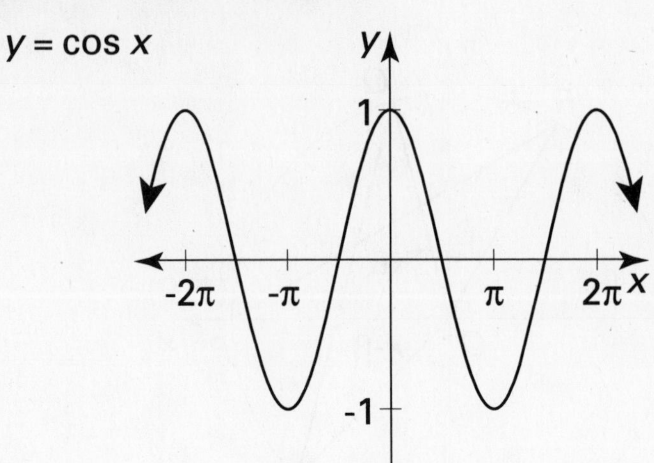

$y = \sin x$

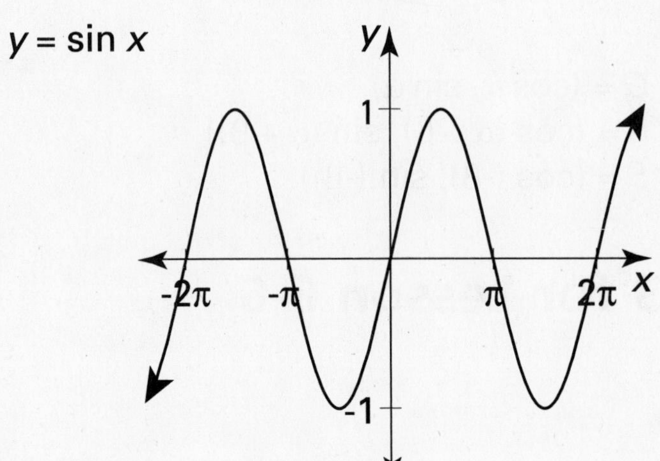

$y = \tan x$

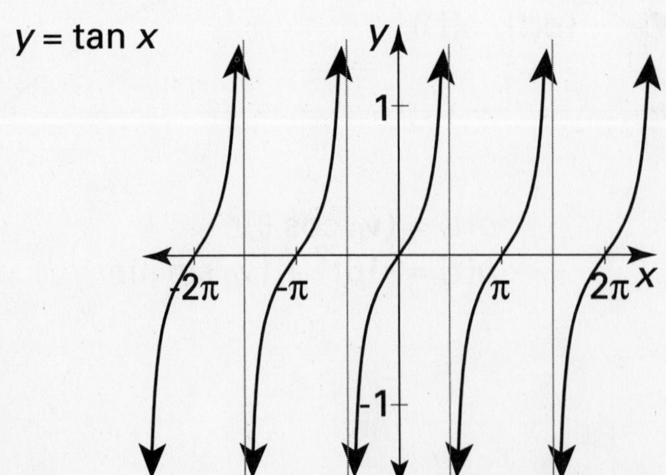

Graphs of the Inverse Sine, Cosine, and Tangent Functions

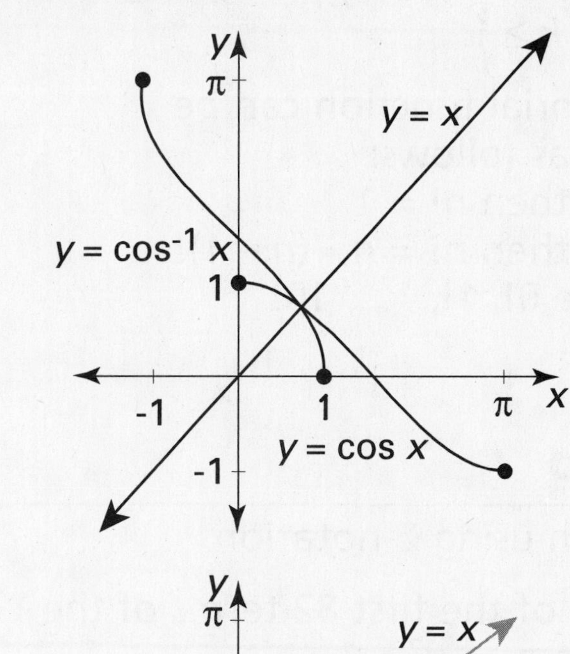

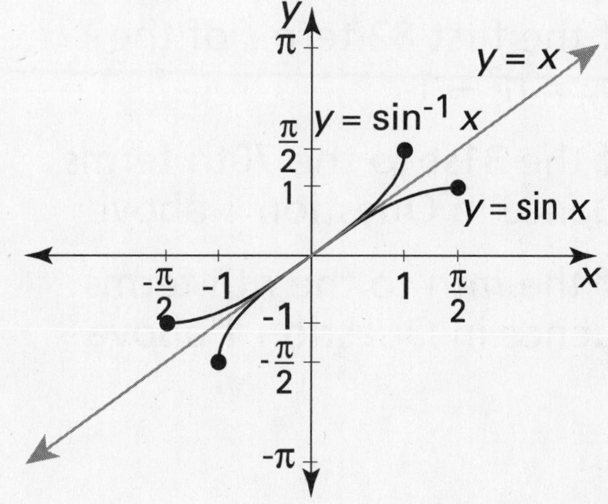

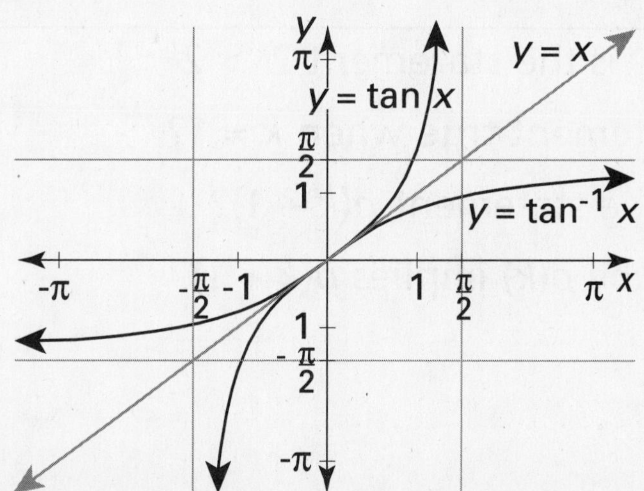

Warm-up

Lesson 7-1

1. List the first ten terms of the sequence defined by $p^k = \lfloor \ln k \rfloor$, for integers $k \geq 1$.

2. The factorial function can be defined as follows:
   If $n = 0$, then $n! = 1$
   If $n > 0$, then $n! = n \cdot (n - 1)!$
   Generate 0!, 1!, . . ., 10!

Warm-up

Lesson 7-2

Express each using Σ-notation.

1. The sum of the first 82 terms of the sequence $a_n = n^2 - 1$

2. The sum of the 31st to the 70th terms of the sequence in Question 1 above

3. The sum of the *m*th to the *n*th terms of the sequence in Question 1 above

Warm-up

Lesson 7-3

Suppose $p(k)$ is the statement $2^k > 2^{k-1}$.

1. Is the statement true when $k = 1$?

2. What is the statement $p(k + 1)$?

3. Explain why $p(k)$ implies $p(k + 1)$.

Warm-up

Lesson 7-4

1. Evaluate the first six terms of the sequence $a_n = 7^n - 1$.
2. What is the largest common factor of these six terms?
3. Prove that every term of the sequence is divisible by that factor.

Warm-up

Lesson 7-5

Let $S(n)$ be the statement $n! > 10^n$.

1. What is the smallest integer k for which $S(k)$ is true?
2. Explain: If $S(k)$ is true, then $S(k + 1)$ must be true.

Warm-up

Lesson 7-6

Consider the sequence defined by $a_n = \frac{3}{11}(1 - (.01)^n)$.

1. Write the first five terms of this sequence.
2. What is $\lim_{n \to \infty} a_n$?

Warm-up

Lesson 7-7

Give a prime factorization of each integer.

1. 360

2. 123,123

3. 10^n

Warm-up

Lesson 7-8

Suppose that you are allowed to switch any two consecutive elements of a sequence. In how many steps can you change 3, 5, 4, 1, 2 into 1, 2, 3, 4, 5? Show each step.

Warm-up

Lesson 7-9

Construct a list of 5 numbers for which the Bubblesort algorithm will require interchanges at each of the 4 passes.

Fibonacci Sequence

January 1			February 1		
1	0	0	0	1	0
A	B	C	A	B	C
	$D = 1$			$D = 1$	
March 1			**April 1**		
1	0	1	1	1	1
A	B	C	A	B	C
	$D = 2$			$D = 3$	
May 1			**June 1**		
2	1	2	3	2	3
A	B	C	A	B	C
	$D = 5$			$D = 8$	

A = number of pairs of rabbits born today

B = number of pairs of rabbits one month old

C = number of pairs of rabbits $\geq$ 2 months old

D = total number of pairs of rabbits

Principles of Mathematical Induction

Principle of Mathematical Induction (Original Form)

Let $S(n)$ be a sentence in n. If
(1) $S(1)$ is true, and
(2) for all integers $k \geq 1$, the assumption that $S(k)$ is true implies that $S(k + 1)$ is true,
then $S(n)$ is true for all positive integers n.

Principle of Mathematical Induction (Strong Form)

Suppose that for each positive integer n, $S(n)$ is a sentence in n. If
(1) $S(1)$ is true, and
(2) for all integers $k \geq 1$, the assumption that $S(1), S(2), \ldots, S(k - 1), S(k)$ are all true implies that $S(k + 1)$ is also true,

then $S(n)$ is true for all integers $n \geq 1$.

Example 1: Bubblesort

Pass 1:

initial order	switch 7 & 3	no switch	switch 11 &1	switch 11 & 9	switch 11 & 4	final order
4	4	4	4	4	4	11
9	9	9	9	9	11	4
1	1	1	1	11	9	9
11	11	11	11	1	1	1
3	3	7	7	7	7	7
7	7	3	3	3	3	3

Pass 2:

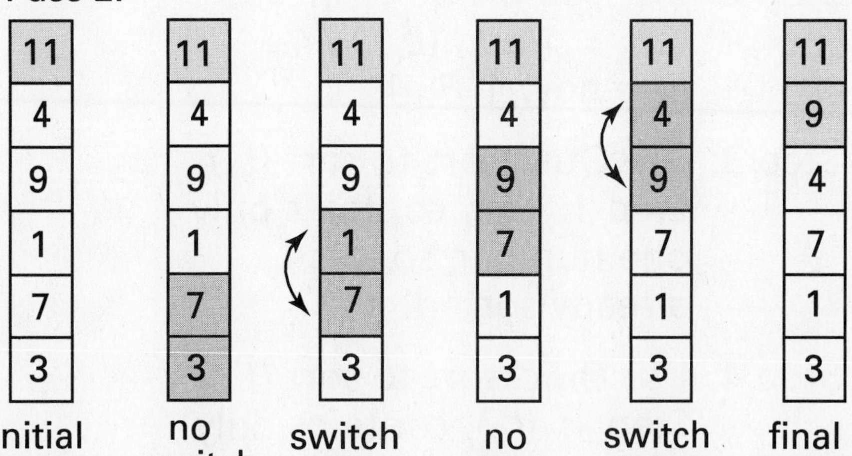

Pass 3:

initial order	switch 3 &1	no switch	switch 7 & 4	final order
11	11	11	11	11
9	9	9	9	9
4	4	4	4	7
7	7	7	7	4
1	1	3	3	3
3	3	1	1	1

Example 2: Quicksort

Step 1: The list L contains more than one number, so continue to Step 2.

Step 2: $f = 7$ so compare 7 with the remaining numbers and group them into two sublists:
$L_\ell = 3, 1, 4$ and $L_r = 11, 9$.
L now looks like 3, 1, 4, 7, 11, 9.

Step 3: Use Quicksort to sort $L_\ell = 3, 1, 4$.
Step 1: L_ℓ contains more than one number, so continue.

Step 2: $f = 3$, so divide L_ℓ into $(L_\ell)_\ell = 1$ and $(L_\ell)_r = 4$.
L_ℓ is now 1, 3, 4.

Step 3: Use Quicksort to sort $(L_\ell)_\ell$.
Step 1: $(L_\ell)_\ell$ contains only one number, so it is already sorted.

Step 4: Use Quicksort to sort $(L_\ell)_r$
Step 1: $(L_\ell)_r$ contains only one number, sort is already sorted.

Now L_ℓ is sorted, and L looks like 1, 3, 4, 7, 11, 9.

Example 2: Quicksort (continued)

Step 4: Use Quicksort to sort $L_r = 11, 9$.
 Step 1: L_r contains more than one number, so continue.
 Step 2: $f = 11$, so divide L_r into $(L_r)_\ell = 9$ and $(L_r)_r$ is empty. L_r is now 9, 11.
 Step 3: Quicksort to sort $(L_r)_\ell$.
  Step 1: $(L_r)_\ell$ contains only one number, so it is already sorted.
 Step 4: Use Quicksort to sort $(L_r)_r$.
  Step 1: $(L_r)_r$ contains no numbers, so it is already sorted.
 Now L_r is sorted, and L looks like 1, 3, 4, 7, 9,11.

Now L is sorted.

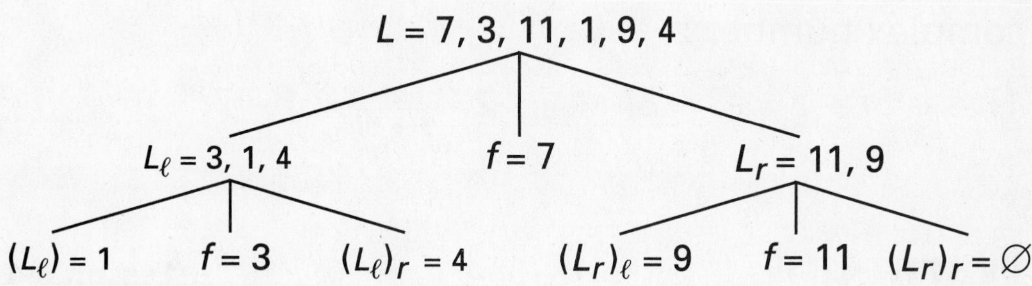

Warm-up

Lesson 8-1

Solve each of these equations.

1. $x^2 + 4x + 3 = 0$

2. $x^2 - 4x + 3 = 0$

3. $x^2 + 2x + 3 = 0$

4. $x^2 + 2x + 10 = 0$

Warm-up

Lesson 8-2

Suppose $A = (1, 0)$ and $B = (0, 0)$. Find the measure of $\angle ABC$ in degrees for the given value of C.

1. $C = (\cos 65°, \sin 65°)$

2. $C = (-2, -2)$

3. $C = (72, -36)$

Warm-up

Lesson 8-3

Solve each of the equations for the complex number z.

1. $4 + 5i + z = -3 - 8i$

2. $\frac{z}{9 + 6i} = 1 - 7i$

Warm-up

Lesson 8-4

Let G_1 be the graph of $y = \sin x$, G_2 be the graph of $y = 2 \sin x$, G_3 be the graph of $y = 2 + \sin x$, and G_4 be the graph of $y = \sin 2x$. Describe how G_2, G_3, and G_4 are related to G_1.

Warm-up

Lesson 8-5

Carefully graph the eleven points (r, θ) satisfying $r = 6 \cos 2\theta$, when $\theta = 0°$, $\pm 10°$, $\pm 20°$, $\pm 30°$, $\pm 40°$ and $\pm 45°$.

Warm-up

Lesson 8-6

Let $z = 2 + 3i$.

1. Calculate z^2, z^3, and z^4.
2. Find the distance of the graphs of z, z^2, z^3, and z^4 from the origin.
3. Predict what the distance of z^5 will be from the origin. Check your prediction by calculating z^5 and its distance from the origin.
4. Generalize Question 3.

Warm-up

Lesson 8-7

Which of the following are 8th roots of 1?

1. 1

2. -1

3. i

4. $-i$

5. $\frac{\sqrt{2} + i\sqrt{2}}{2}$

6. $\cos 60° + i \sin 60°$

7. $1 - i$

8. $[1, 225°]$

Warm-up

Lesson 8-8

1. Find all solutions to the equation $(2x + 25)(x^2 + x + 6) = 0$.
2. Find a 3rd degree polynomial equation that has the same solutions as the equation of Question 1.

Warm-up

Lesson 8-9

1. Find all solutions to the equation $x^3 + x^2 + x + 1 = 0$.
2. Write a polynomial equation whose zeros are 1, -1, i, and $-i$.

Warm-up

Lesson 8-10

Enter 3 into your calculator set to radians. Repeatedly press the sine key, writing down the values you get rounded to the nearest thousandth.

1. Give a recursive definition for the sequence you are creating.
2. Conjecture the limit of the nth term of this sequence as $n \to \infty$.

Polar Grid

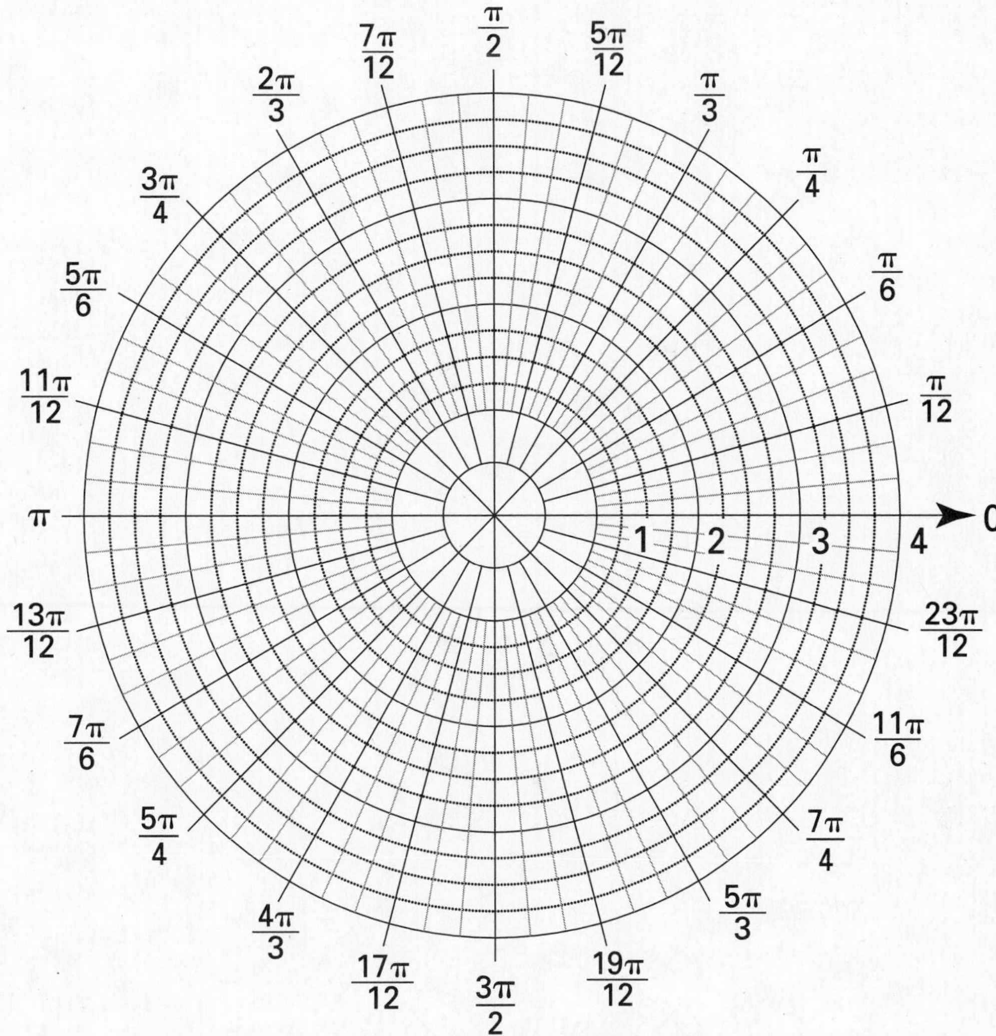

$\frac{\pi}{2}$
$\frac{5\pi}{12}$
$\frac{\pi}{3}$
$\frac{\pi}{4}$
$\frac{\pi}{6}$
$\frac{\pi}{12}$
0
1
2
3
4
$\frac{23\pi}{12}$
$\frac{11\pi}{6}$
$\frac{7\pi}{4}$
$\frac{5\pi}{3}$
$\frac{19\pi}{12}$
$\frac{3\pi}{2}$
$\frac{17\pi}{12}$
$\frac{4\pi}{3}$
$\frac{5\pi}{4}$
$\frac{7\pi}{6}$
$\frac{13\pi}{12}$
π
$\frac{11\pi}{12}$
$\frac{5\pi}{6}$
$\frac{3\pi}{4}$
$\frac{2\pi}{3}$
$\frac{7\pi}{12}$

Polar Grids

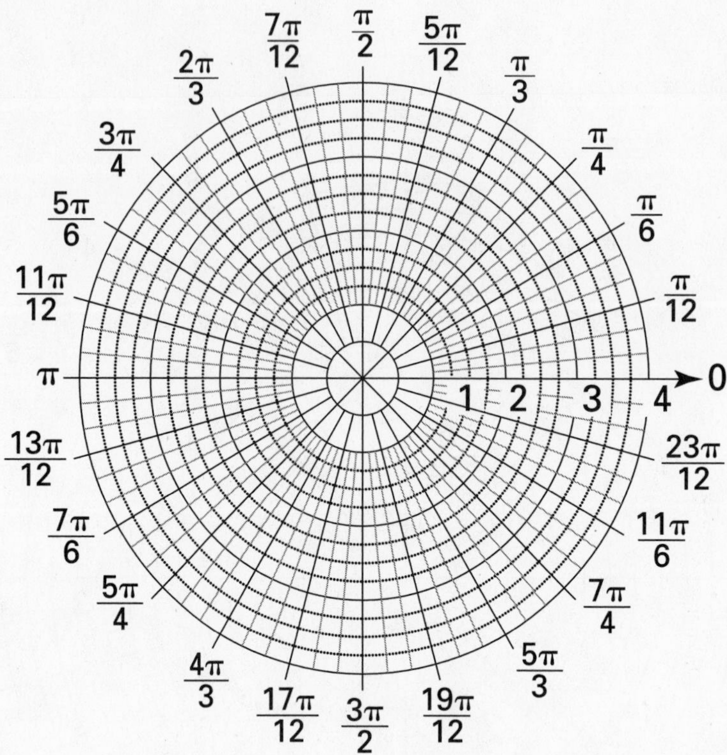
$\frac{7\pi}{12}$
$\frac{\pi}{2}$
$\frac{5\pi}{12}$
$\frac{2\pi}{3}$
$\frac{\pi}{3}$
$\frac{3\pi}{4}$
$\frac{\pi}{4}$
$\frac{5\pi}{6}$
$\frac{\pi}{6}$
$\frac{11\pi}{12}$
$\frac{\pi}{12}$
π
0
1
2
3
4
$\frac{13\pi}{12}$
$\frac{23\pi}{12}$
$\frac{7\pi}{6}$
$\frac{11\pi}{6}$
$\frac{5\pi}{4}$
$\frac{7\pi}{4}$
$\frac{4\pi}{3}$
$\frac{5\pi}{3}$
$\frac{17\pi}{12}$
$\frac{3\pi}{2}$
$\frac{19\pi}{12}$

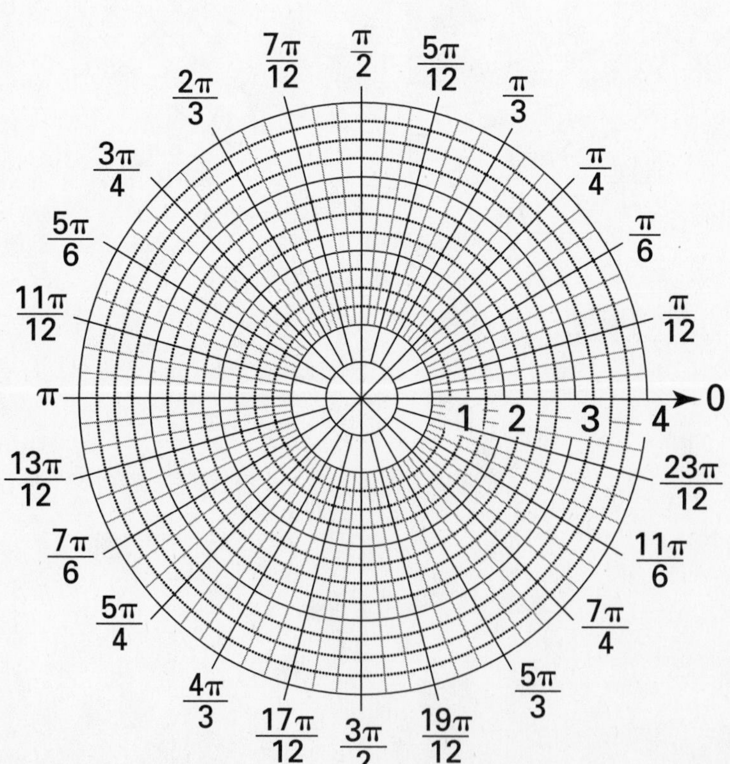
$\frac{7\pi}{12}$
$\frac{\pi}{2}$
$\frac{5\pi}{12}$
$\frac{2\pi}{3}$
$\frac{\pi}{3}$
$\frac{3\pi}{4}$
$\frac{\pi}{4}$
$\frac{5\pi}{6}$
$\frac{\pi}{6}$
$\frac{11\pi}{12}$
$\frac{\pi}{12}$
π
0
1
2
3
4
$\frac{13\pi}{12}$
$\frac{23\pi}{12}$
$\frac{7\pi}{6}$
$\frac{11\pi}{6}$
$\frac{5\pi}{4}$
$\frac{7\pi}{4}$
$\frac{4\pi}{3}$
$\frac{5\pi}{3}$
$\frac{17\pi}{12}$
$\frac{3\pi}{2}$
$\frac{19\pi}{12}$

Example 1

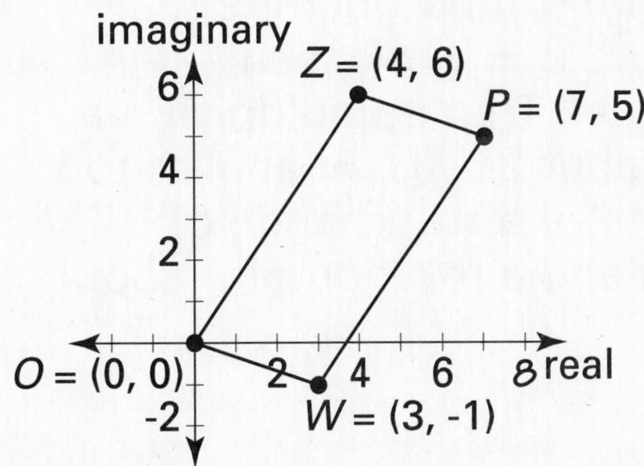

Geometric Addition Theorem

Let $z = a + bi$ and $w = c + di$ be two complex numbers that are not collinear with (0, 0). Then the point representing $z + w$ is the fourth vertex of a parallelogram with consecutive vertices $z = a + bi$, 0, and $w = c + di$.

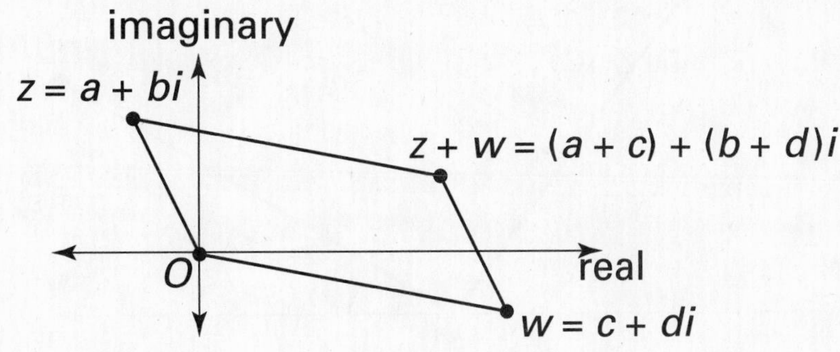

Geometric Multiplication Theorem

Let z and w be complex numbers.
If $z = [r, \theta]$ and $w = [s, \phi]$, then $zw = [rs, \theta + \phi]$. That is, multiplying a complex number z by $[s, \phi]$ applies to z the composite of a size change of magnitude s and a rotation of ϕ about the origin.

In general, multiplication of $z = [r, \theta]$ by $w = [s, \phi]$

(1) produces a size change on z of magnitude s, because the absolute value of z is r and the absolute of the product is rs, and

(2) rotates z through ϕ units, because an argument of z is θ and an argument of product is $\theta + \phi$.

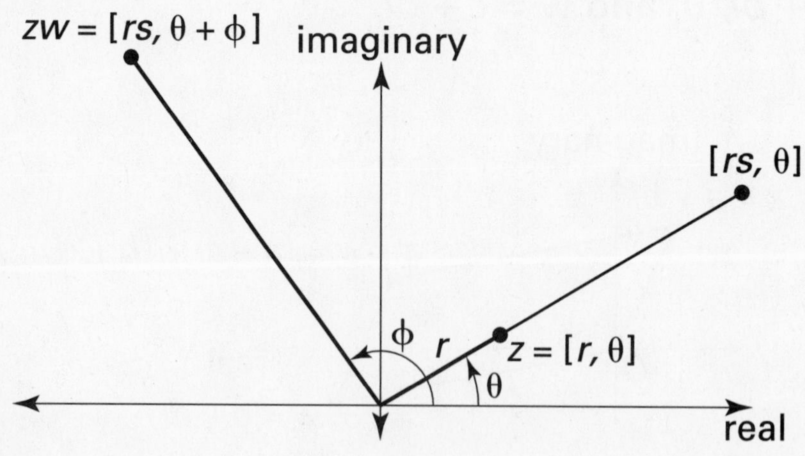

Example 3

θ	0	$\frac{\pi}{4}$	$\frac{\pi}{2}$	$\frac{3\pi}{4}$	π	$\frac{5\pi}{4}$	$\frac{3\pi}{2}$	$\frac{7\pi}{4}$	2π
r	1	$1 + \sqrt{2}$	3	$1 + \sqrt{2}$	1	$1 - \sqrt{2}$	-1	$1 - \sqrt{2}$	1

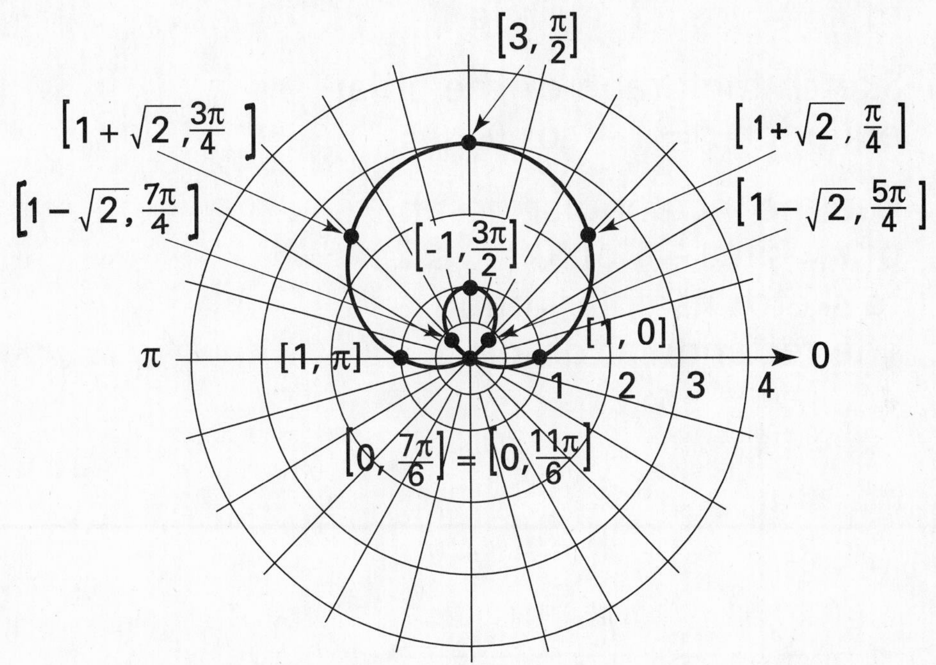

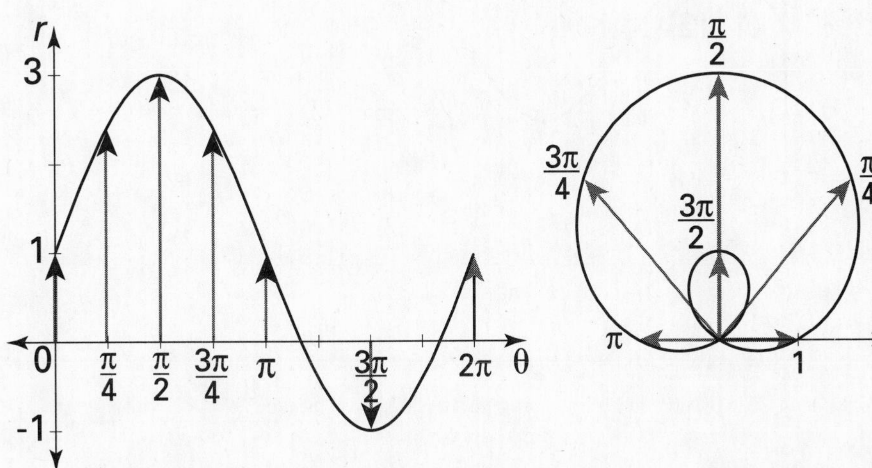

rectangular graph of
$r = 1 + 2 \sin \theta$
$0 \leq \theta \leq 2\pi$

polar graph of
$r = 1 + 2 \sin \theta$
$0 \leq \theta \leq 2\pi$

Additional Examples

1. Sketch the polar equation $r = 4 \cos \theta$.
2. Verify that the polar graph of $r = 4 \cos \theta$ is a circle.
3. Sketch the graph of the polar equation $r = 1 + \cos \theta$.
4. Use the rectangular graph of $r = \sin \theta - 1$ on $0 \le \theta \le 2\pi$ to sketch its polar graph. The rectangular graph is:

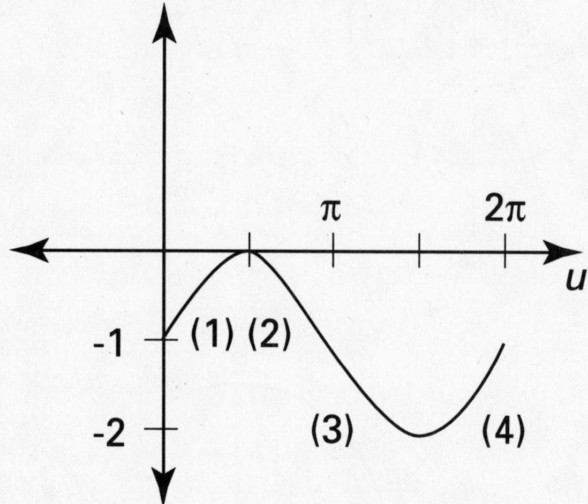

Example 1

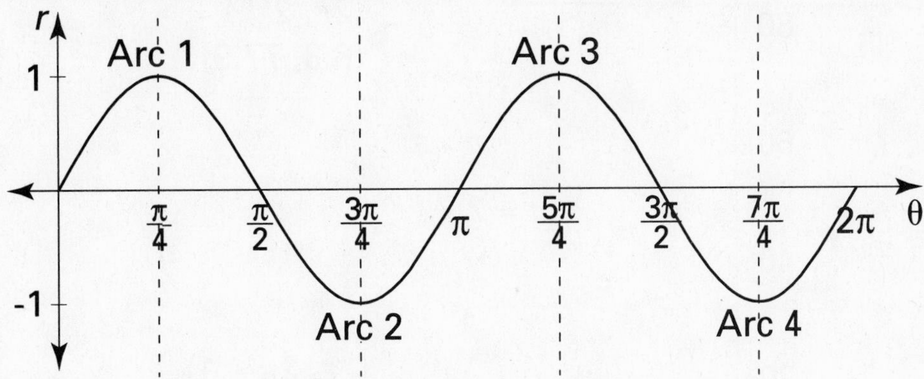
r
1
-1
Arc 1
Arc 2
Arc 3
Arc 4
$\frac{\pi}{4}$
$\frac{\pi}{2}$
$\frac{3\pi}{4}$
π
$\frac{5\pi}{4}$
$\frac{3\pi}{2}$
$\frac{7\pi}{4}$
2π
θ

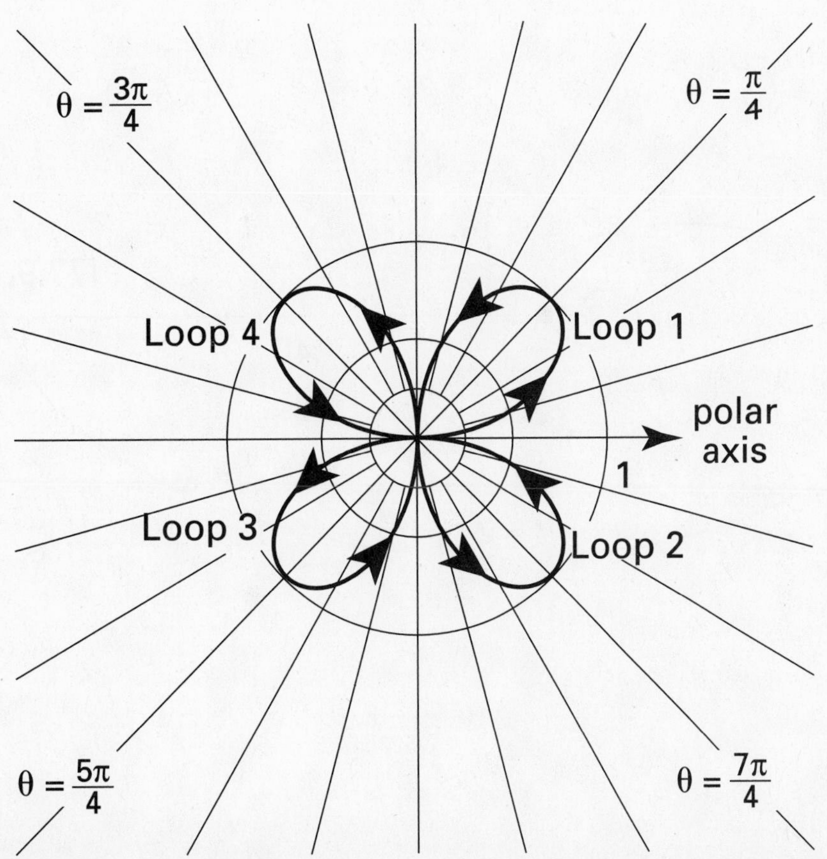
$\theta = \frac{3\pi}{4}$
$\theta = \frac{\pi}{4}$
Loop 4
Loop 1
polar axis
1
Loop 3
Loop 2
$\theta = \frac{5\pi}{4}$
$\theta = \frac{7\pi}{4}$

Example 2

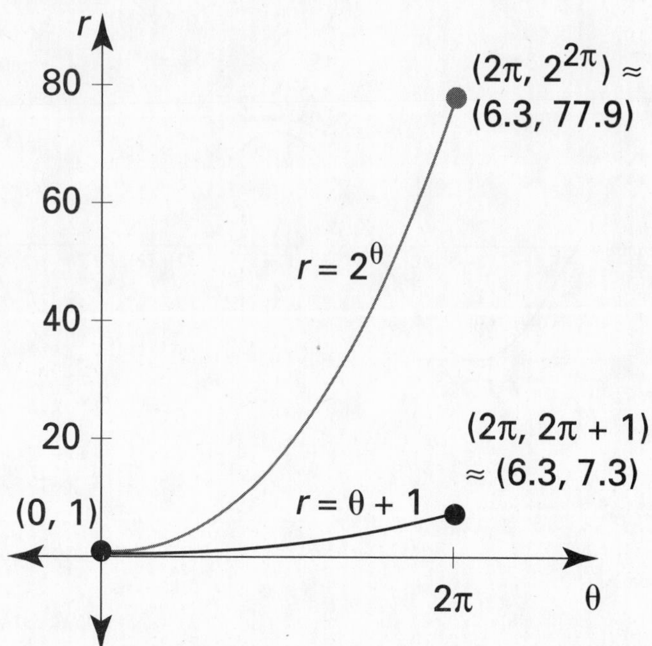
r
80
60
40
20
$(2\pi, 2^{2\pi}) \approx$
(6.3, 77.9)
$r = 2^{\theta}$
$(2\pi, 2\pi + 1)$
$\approx (6.3, 7.3)$
$r = \theta + 1$
(0, 1)
2π
θ

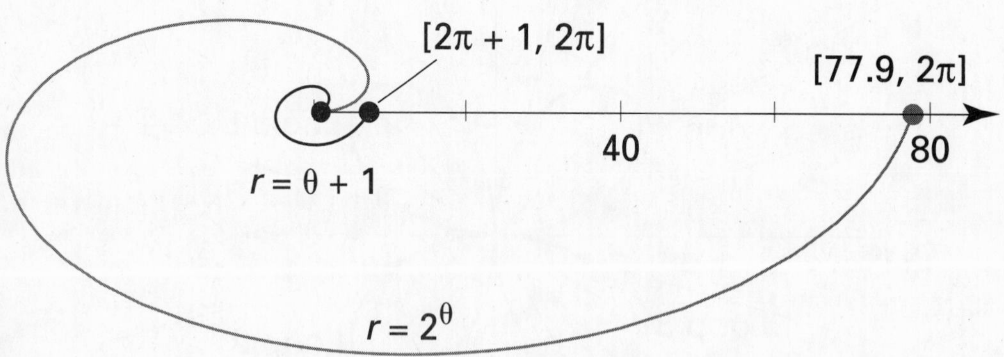
$[2\pi + 1, 2\pi]$
$[77.9, 2\pi]$
40
80
$r = \theta + 1$
$r = 2^{\theta}$

Graphs of Powers of Complex Numbers

Powers of $z = [1.1, \frac{\pi}{3}]$

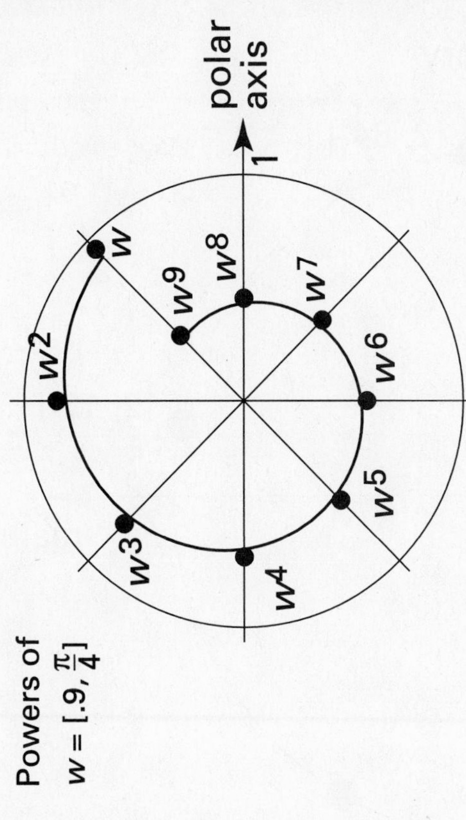

Powers of $w = [.9, \frac{\pi}{4}]$

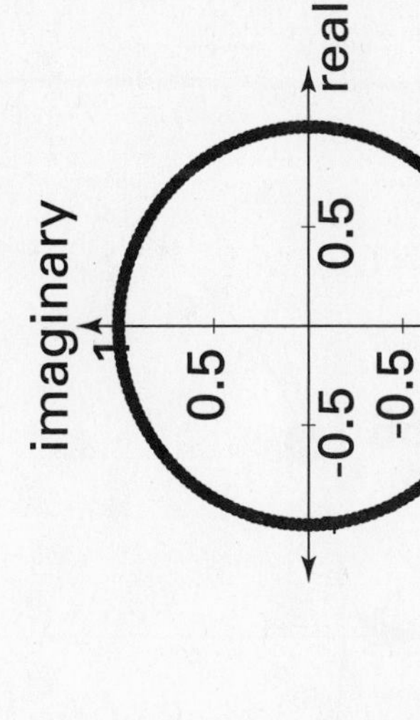
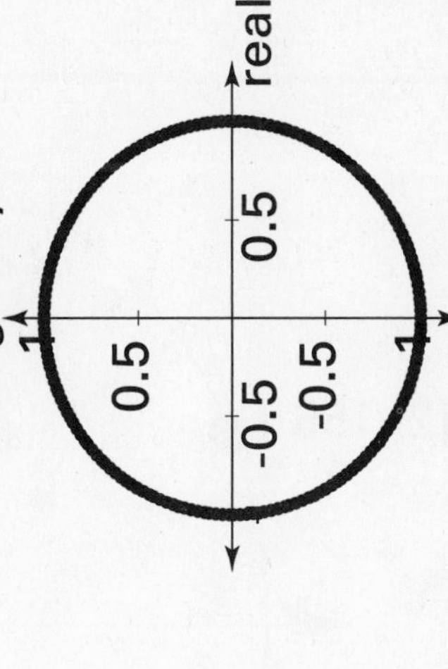

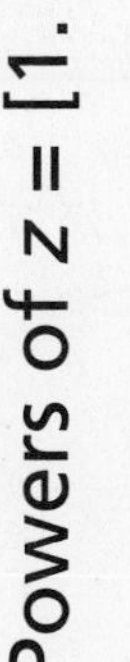

Powers of $z = [1. 1]$

$\{z^n : z^n = \cos n + i \sin n, 1 \le n \le 10\}$

$\{z^n : z^n = \cos n + i \sin n, 1 \le n \le 50\}$

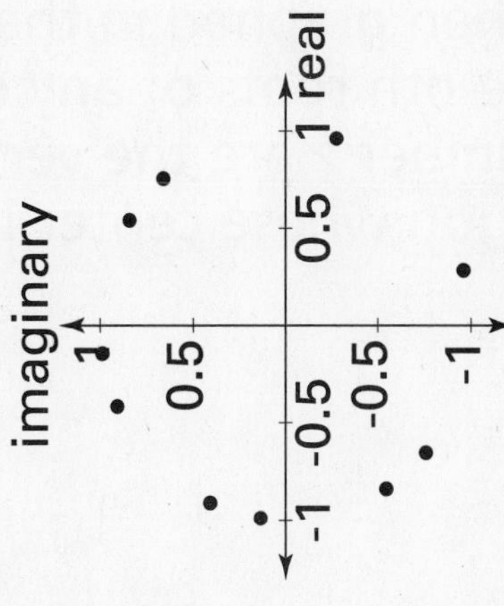

$\{z^n : z^n = \cos n + i \sin n, 1 \le n \le 500\}$

Example 2

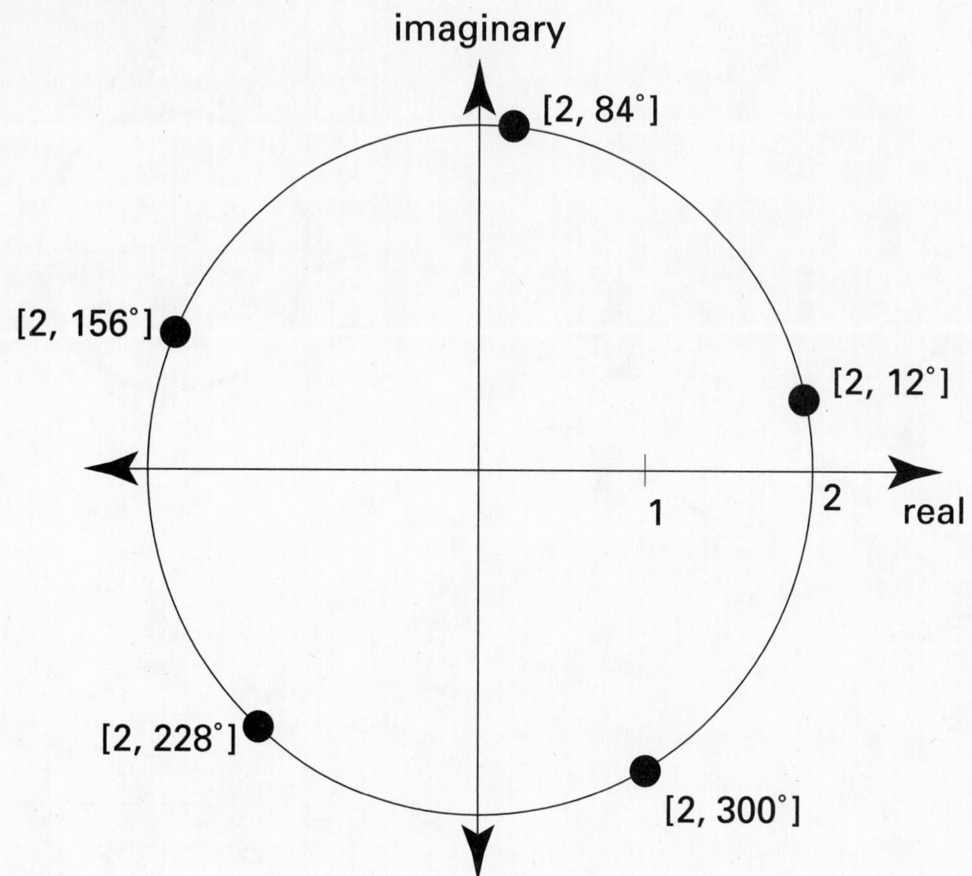

Geometric *n*th Roots Theorem

When graphed in the complex plane, the *n*th roots of any nonzero complex number *z* are the vertices of a regular *n*-gon whose center is at (0, 0).

*n*th Roots of Real Numbers

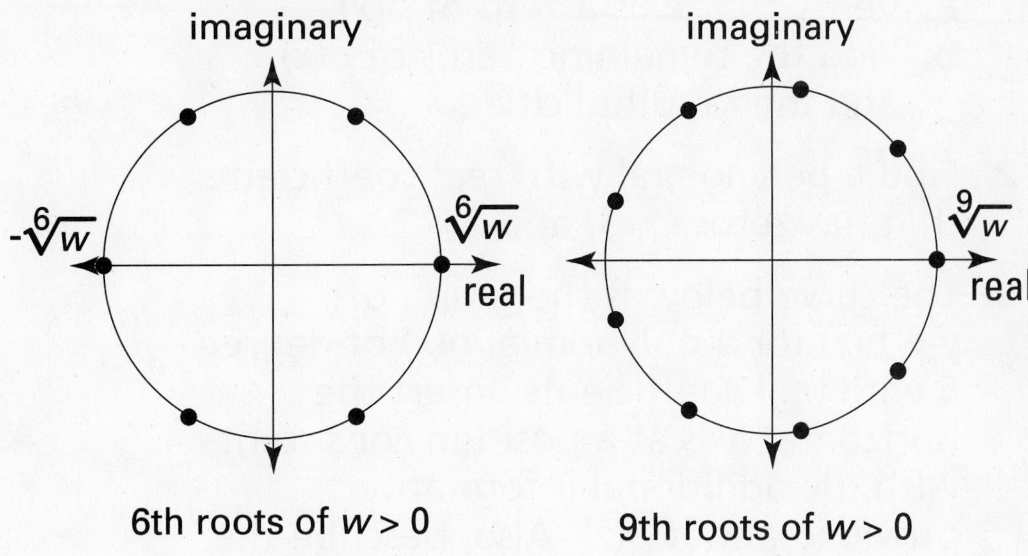

6th roots of $w > 0$

9th roots of $w > 0$

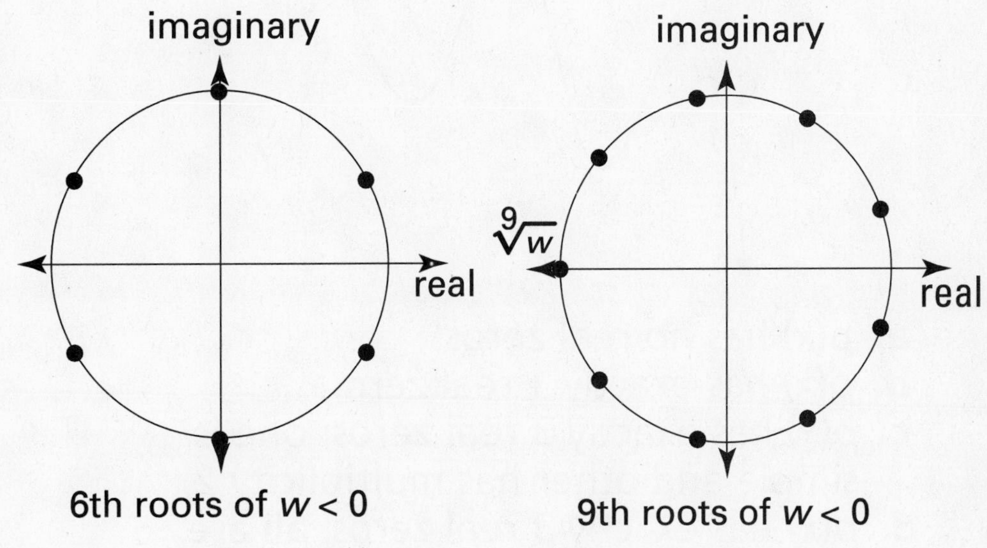

6th roots of $w < 0$

9th roots of $w < 0$

Additional Examples

1. Let $p(x) = x^6 - 5x^5 + 10x^4 - 20x^3 + 24x^2$.
   a. Verify that $2i$ is a zero of $p(x)$.
   b. Find the remaining zeros of $p(x)$ and their multiplicities.

2. Find a polynomial with real coefficients that has zeros -1, 3, and $2 + 3i$.

3. The curve below is the graph of $y = p(x)$ for a polynomial $p(x)$ of degree 5 with real coefficients. Insert the horizontal axis at a position consistent with the additional information provided about $p(x)$. Also, describe the nonreal zeros.

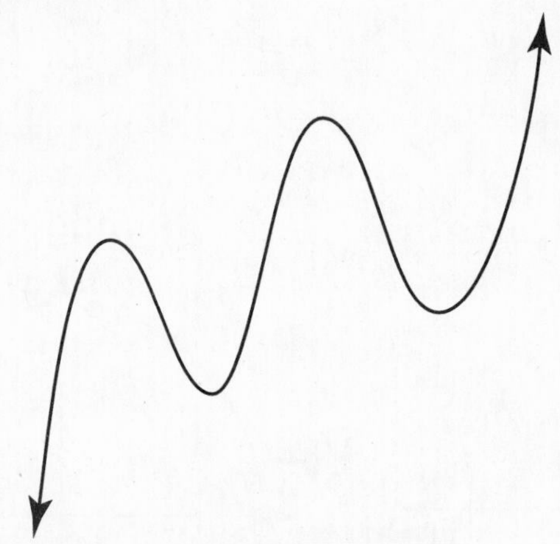

   a. $p(x)$ has no real zeros.
   b. $p(x)$ has exactly 1 real zero.
   c. $p(x)$ has exactly 3 real zeros; one is simple and other has multiplicity 2.
   d. $p(x)$ has exactly 3 real zeros, all are simple zeros.
   e. $p(x)$ has exactly 4 real, simple zeros.
   f. $p(x)$ has 5 real, simple zeros. There are no other zeros.

Graphs

$$p(x) = 4x^4 + 8x^3 - 3x^2 - 9x + c$$

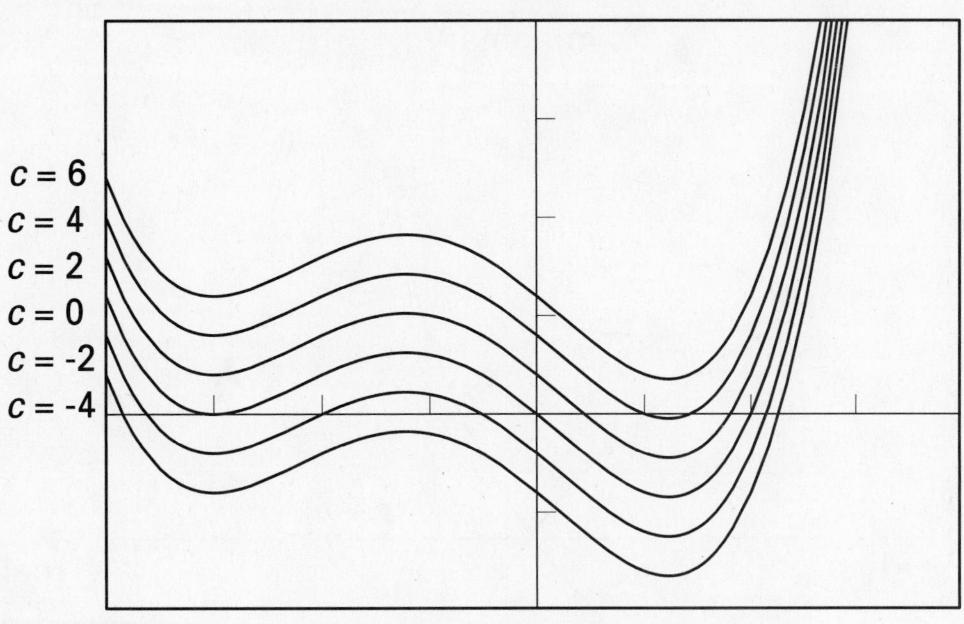

$-2 \le x \le 2$, x-scale = 0.5

$-10 \le y \le 20$, y-scale = 5

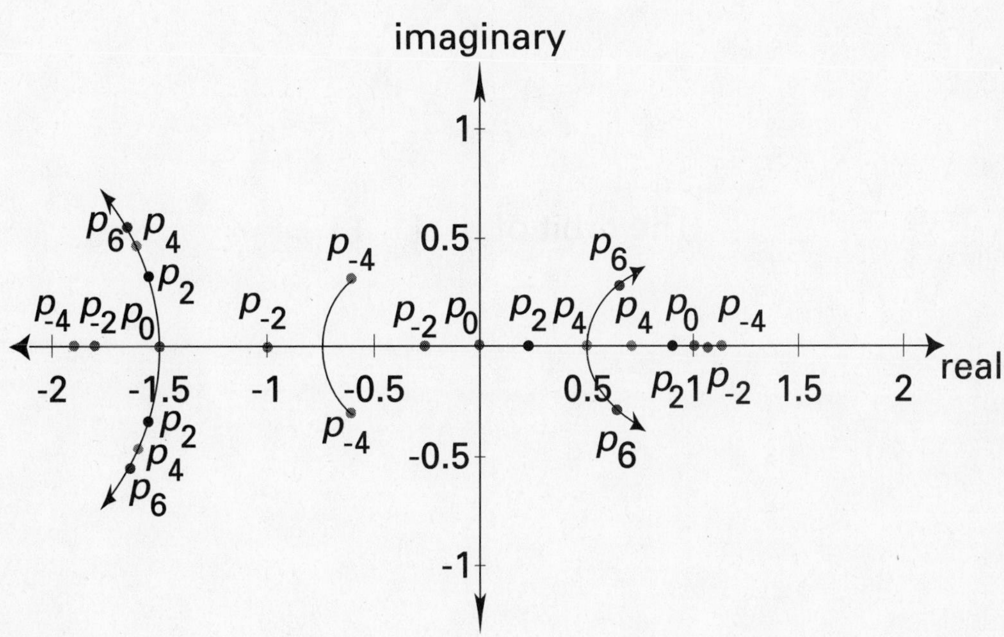

Orbit of [1, 18°] when $f(z) = z^2$

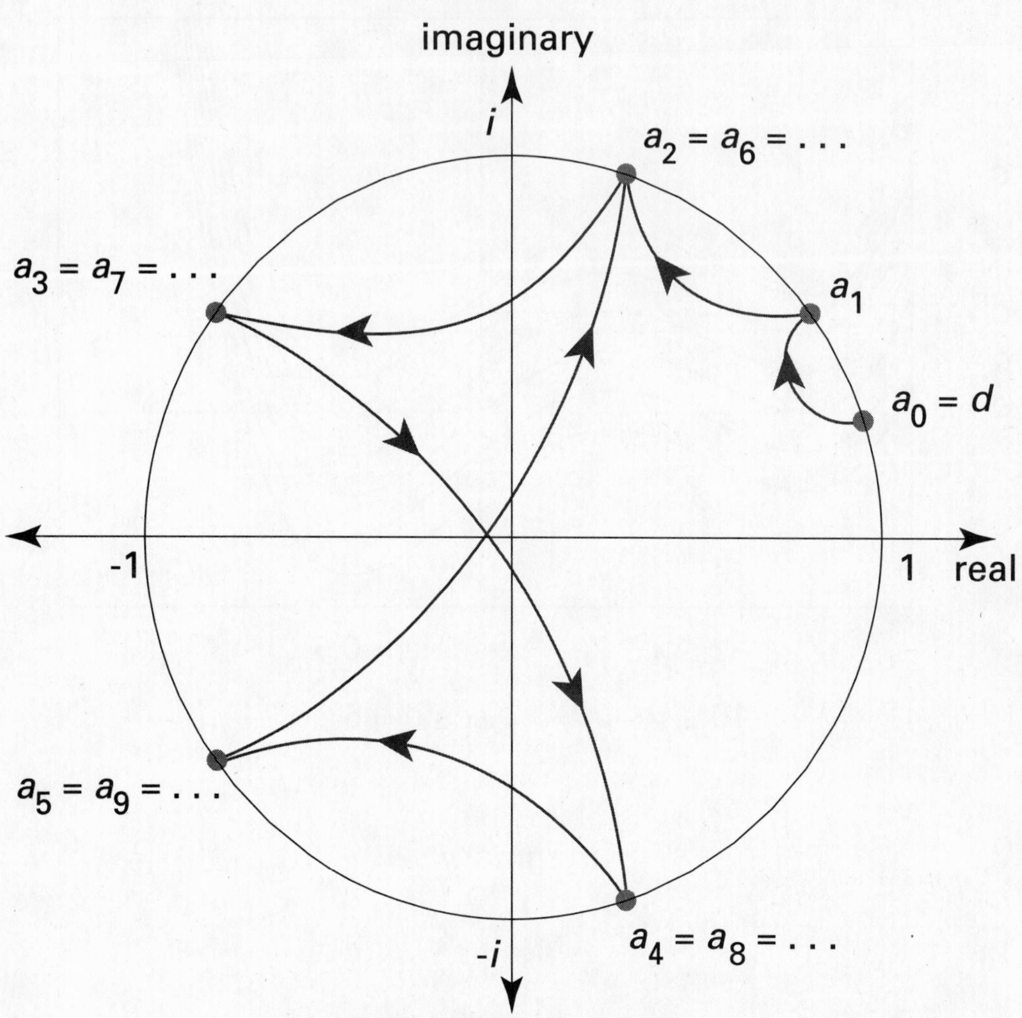

The orbit of $d = [1, 18°]$.

Warm-up

Lesson 9-1

In Houston, on March 1, the sun sets at 6:20 P.M. On April 1, the sun sets at 6:40 P.M. By how many minutes per day does sunset get later during the month of March?

Warm-up

Lesson 9-2

Suppose $g(x) = 5x^2 - 12x$. Calculate each of the following.

1. $g(x + \Delta x)$

2. $g(x + \Delta x) - g(x)$

3. $\dfrac{g(x + \Delta x) - g(x)}{\Delta x}$

4. $\lim\limits_{\Delta x \to 0} \dfrac{g(x + \Delta x) - g(x)}{\Delta x}$

Warm-up

Lesson 9-3

Work with the same classmate you were paired with for the In-class Activity on page 568 in the Student Edition. Fill in the chart below with the values you found from Parts 3 and 4 of the activity. Then plot the points of the function f'.

x	$f(x) = \sin x$	$f'(x)$

Warm-up

Lesson 9-4

Listed here are the highest Dow-Jones stock averages for each year from 1962 to 1982. In which year was the highest rate of change per year of the yearly rate of change?

1962	726.01	1969	968.85	1976	1014.79
1963	767.21	1970	842.00	1977	999.75
1964	891.71	1971	950.82	1978	907.74
1965	969.26	1972	1036.27	1979	897.61
1966	995.15	1973	1051.70	1980	1000.17
1967	943.08	1974	891.66	1981	1024.05
1968	985.21	1975	881.81	1982	1070.55

(Source: *The World Almanac and Book of Facts* 1998, p. 127)

Warm-up

Lesson 9-5

1. Consider the quadratic function q with $q(x) = 9x^2 - 27x + 12$.
   a. Use the Derivative of a Quadratic Function formula to determine a formula for q'.
   b. For what values of x is $q'(x) > 0$?
   c. Graph q. From the graph of q, for what values of x is q an increasing function?
   d. Compare your answers to parts b and c.

Warm-up

Lesson 9-6

Estimate the slope of the tangent to the graph of $y = e^x$ at the point $(3, e^3)$ by calculating the slope determined by the points $(3, e^3)$ and $(3 + k, e^{3+k})$, where k is very close to zero.

Length of Day Table and Graph

Length of day (in minutes) on first day of month at 50° north latitude

Date	Day of year	Length
January 1	1	490
February 1	32	560
March 1	60	659
April 1	91	775
May 1	121	882
June 1	152	964
July 1	182	977
August 1	213	913
September 1	244	809
October 1	274	698
November 1	305	587
December 1	335	504

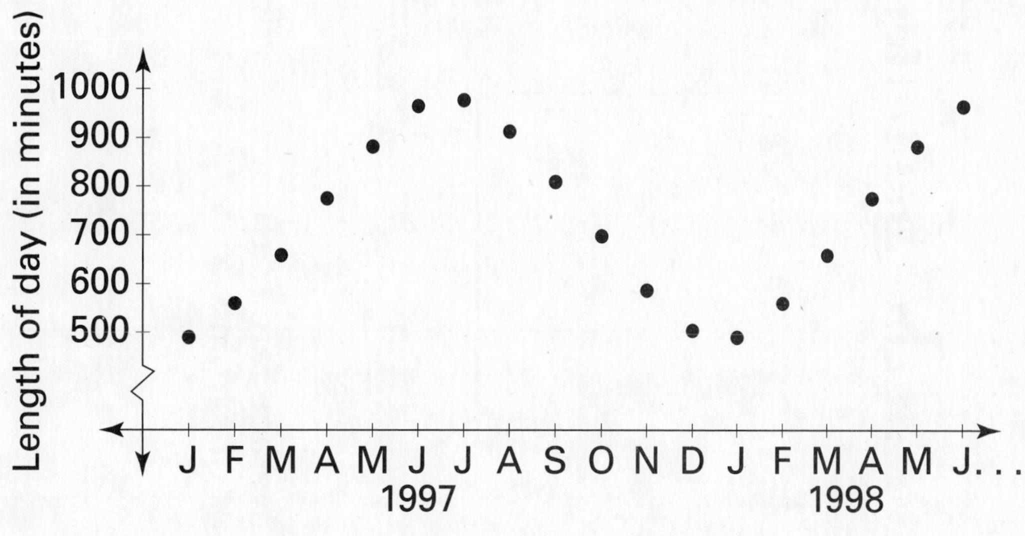

Secant Line and Difference Quotient

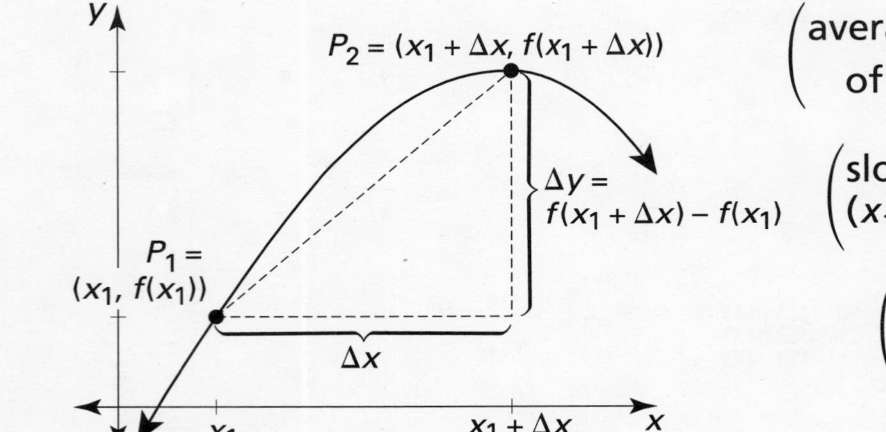

$$\left(\begin{array}{c}\text{average rate of change}\\ \text{of } f \text{ from } x_1 \text{ to } x_2\end{array}\right) = \frac{\Delta y}{\Delta x}$$

$$\left(\begin{array}{c}\text{slope of line through}\\ (x_1, y_1) \text{ and } (x_2, y_2)\end{array}\right) = \frac{y_2 - y_1}{x_2 - x_1} = \frac{f(x_2) - f(x_1)}{x_2 - x_1}$$

$$\left(\begin{array}{c}\text{different quotient}\\ \text{of } f \text{ from } x_1 \text{ to } x_2\end{array}\right) = \frac{f(x_2 + \Delta x) - f(x_1)}{\Delta x}$$

$$\left(\begin{array}{c}\text{average rate of change}\\ \text{of } f \text{ from } x_1 \text{ to } x_2\end{array}\right) = \left(\begin{array}{c}\text{slope of line through}\\ (x_1, y_1) \text{ and } (x_2, y_2)\end{array}\right) = \left(\begin{array}{c}\text{difference quotient}\\ \text{of } f \text{ from } x_1 \text{ to } x_2\end{array}\right)$$

$$\frac{\Delta y}{\Delta x} = \frac{y_2 - y_1}{x_2 - x_1} = \frac{f(x_2) - f(x_1)}{x_2 - x_1} = \frac{f(x_2 + \Delta x) - f(x_1)}{\Delta x}$$

Questions 5–9 and 21

5–9.

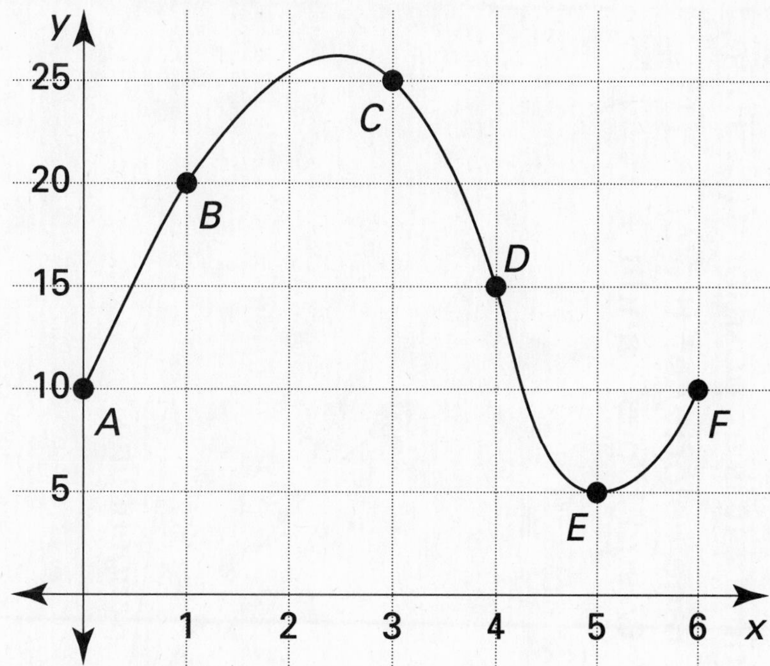

21.

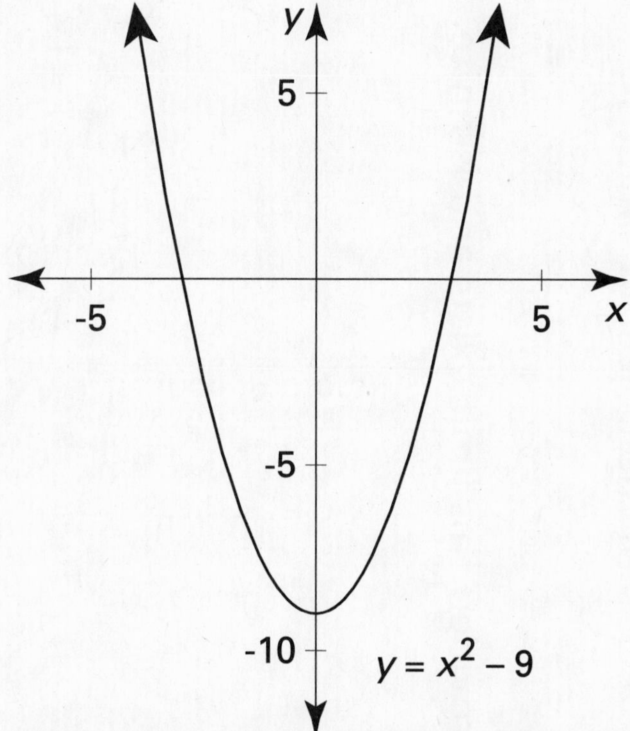

Instantaneous Velocity

Definition

Suppose an object is moving so that at each time t it is at position $f(t)$. Then,

$$\begin{pmatrix}\textbf{instantaneous velocity}\\ \text{of the object at time } t\end{pmatrix} = \lim_{\Delta t \to 0}\begin{pmatrix}\text{average velocity of the object}\\ \text{between times } t \text{ and } t + \Delta t\end{pmatrix}$$

$$= \lim_{\Delta t \to 0} \frac{f(t + \Delta t) - f(t)}{\Delta t},$$

provided this limit exists and is finite.

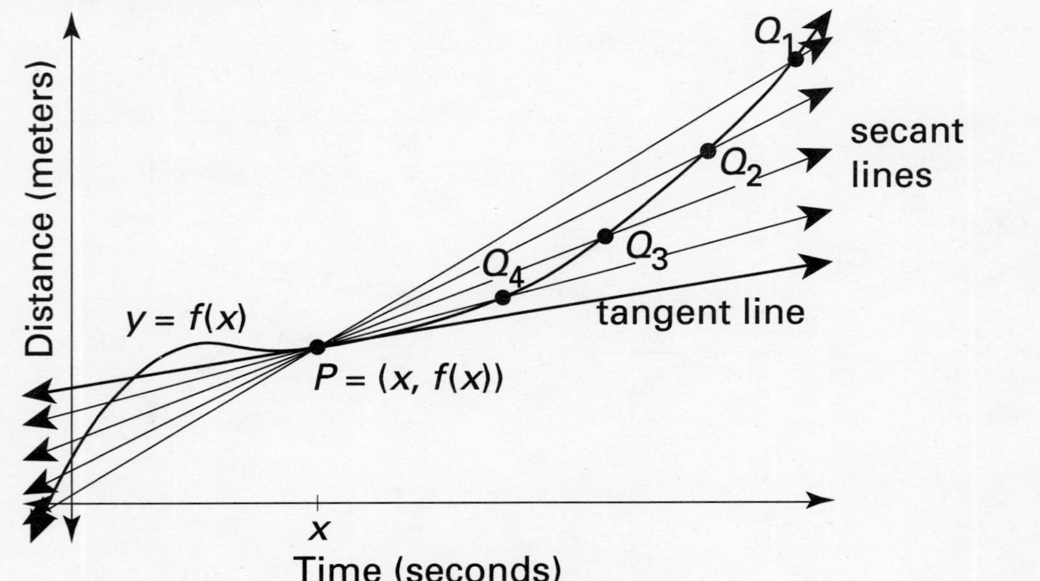

Example 2

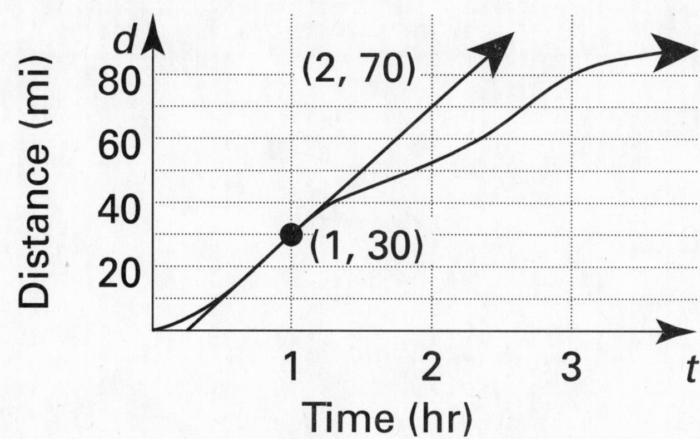

Example 3

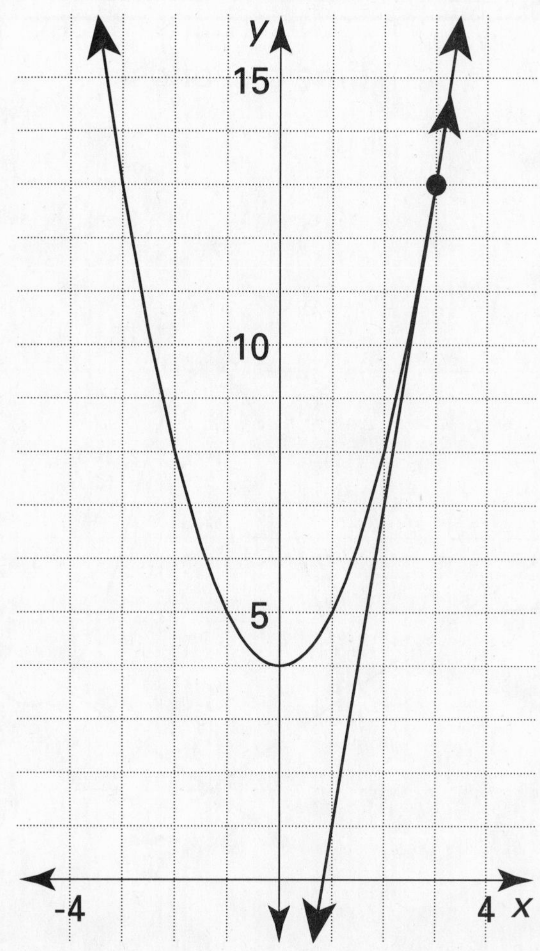

Questions 2 and 6

2.

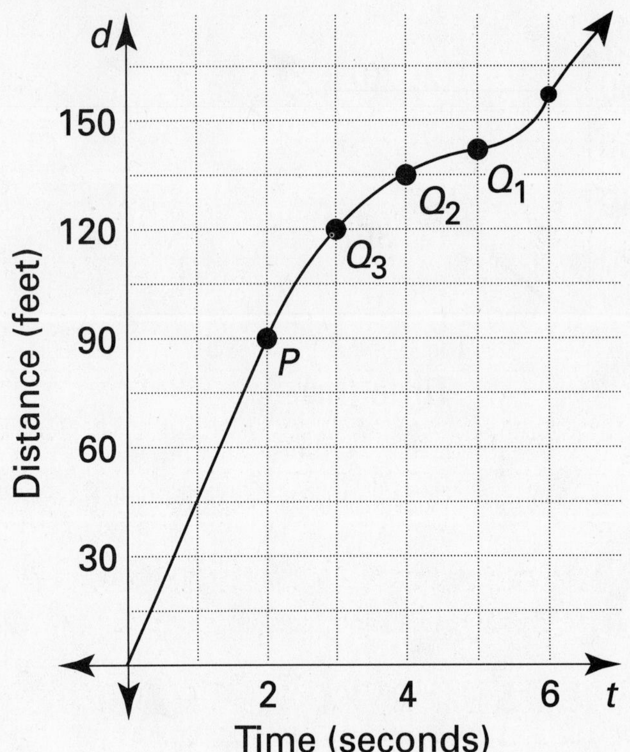

6.

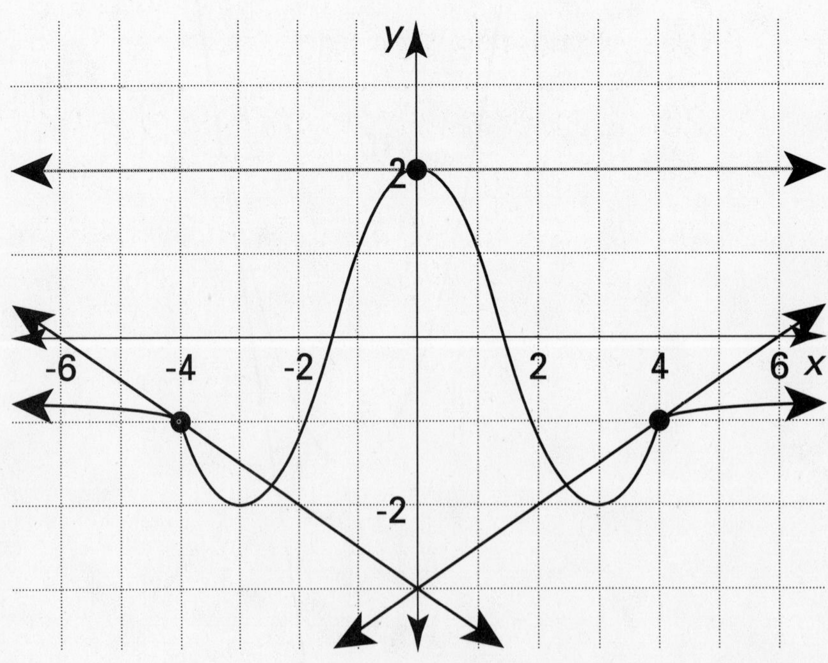

Questions 10, 12 and 13

10.

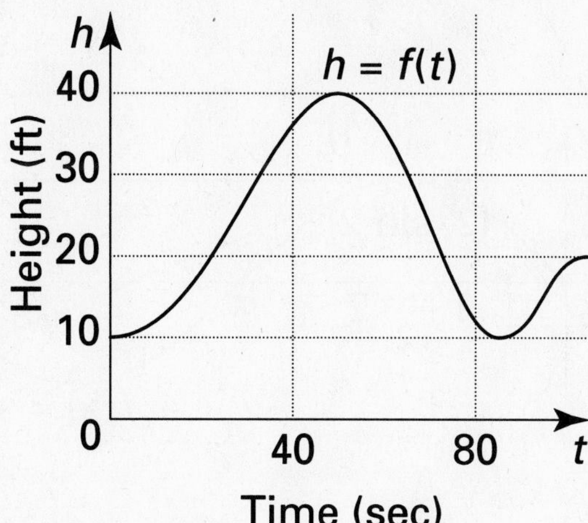

12.

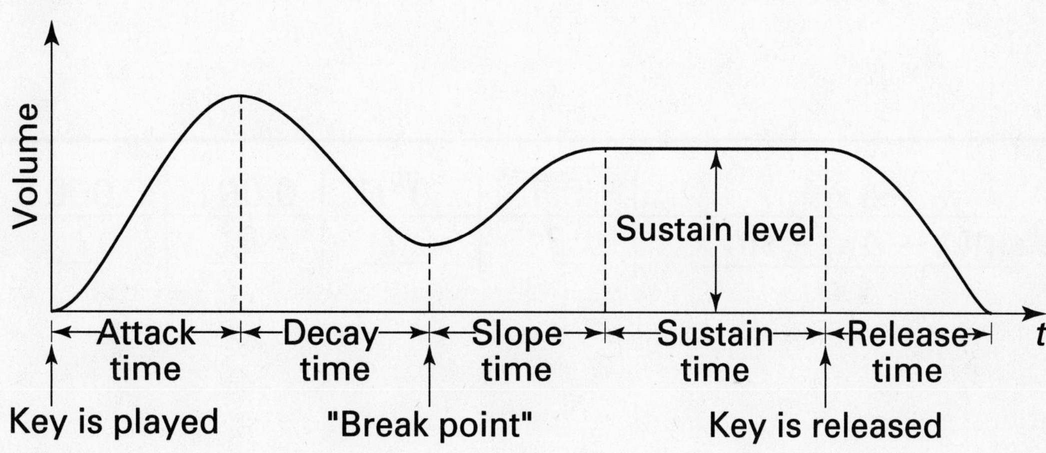

13.

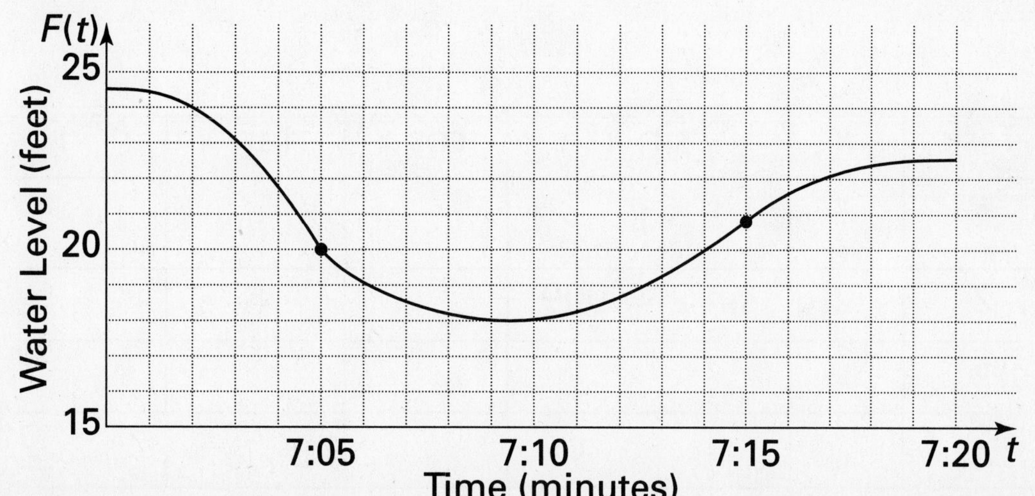

Graph of Sine Function and Tables

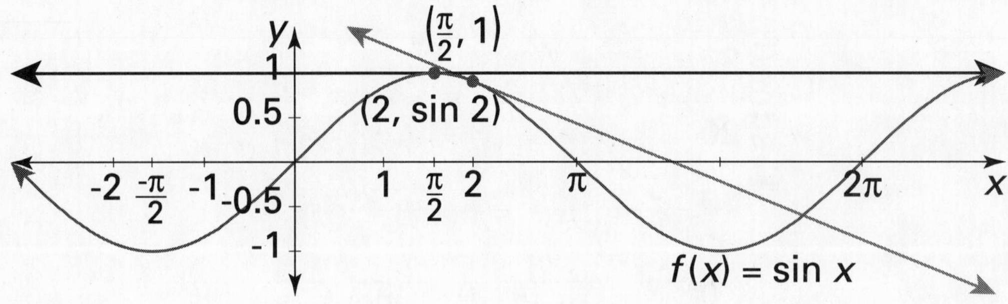

Δx	0.1	0.01	0.001	0.0001
$\frac{\sin(x + \Delta x) - \sin x}{\Delta x}$	?	?	?	?

Task	x	$\sin x$	$\cos x$	$\tan x$	$f'(x)$
1	$\frac{\pi}{2}$	1			
2	2	$\sin 2 \approx .909$			
3					
4					

Example 2

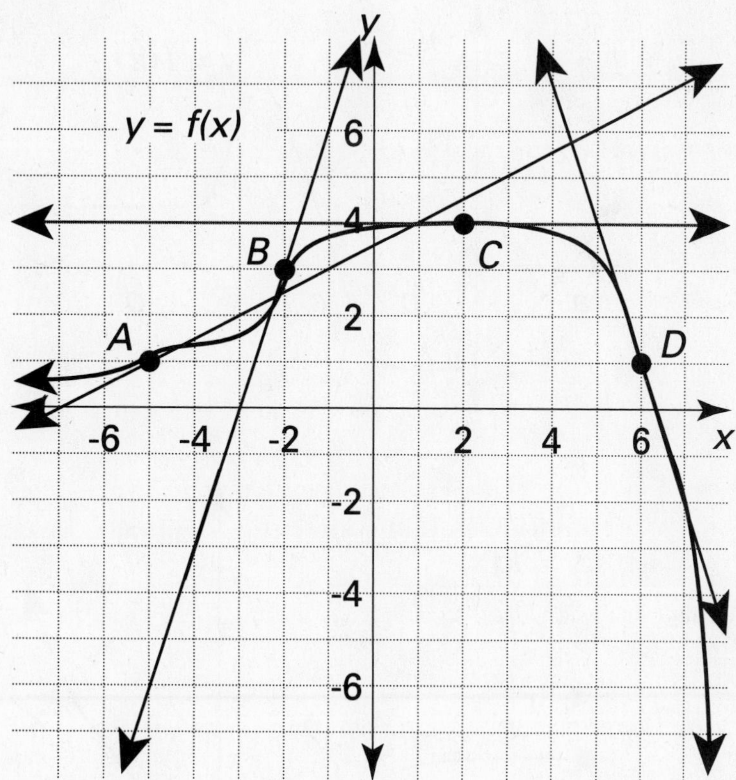

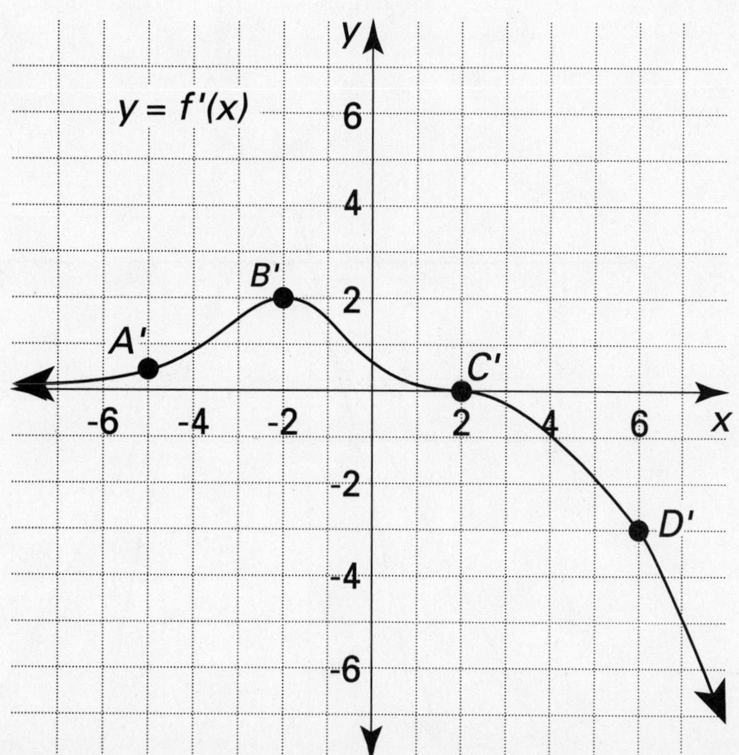

Questions 2, 5, and 11

2.

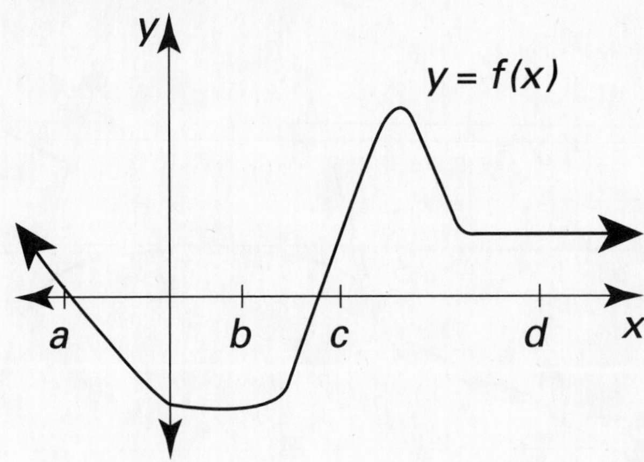

5.

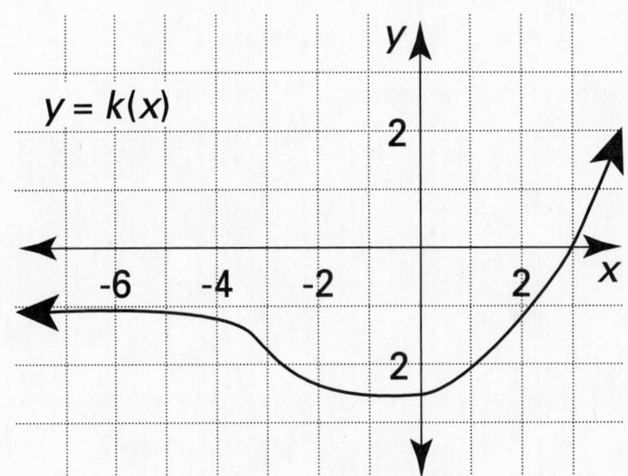

11.

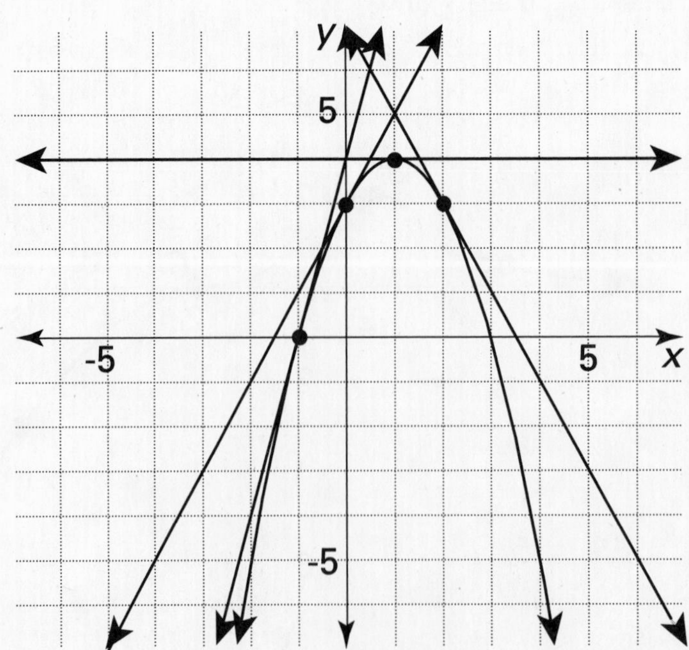

Questions 15, 16, 19, and 20

15.

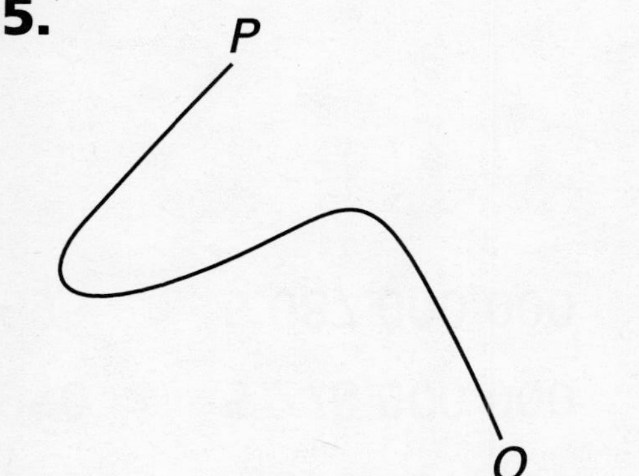

Time

Time

16.

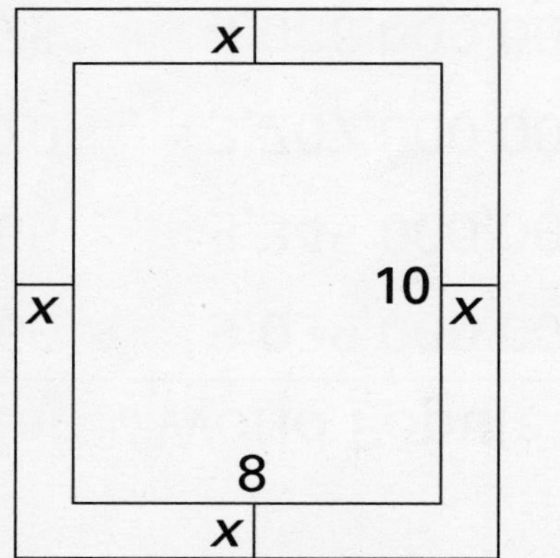

19.

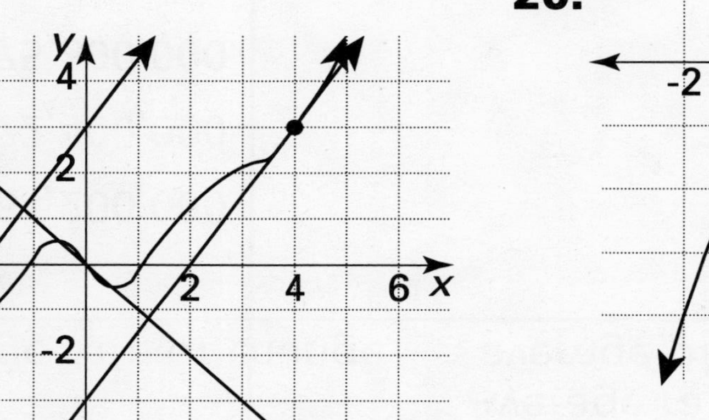

20.

y
-2
2
x
-2
-4

Change in World Population

Year	World Population	Average rate of change	Average rate of change of average of rate of change
1960	3,039,000,000		
1965	3,345,000,000	61,200,000	
1970	3,707,000,000	72,400,000	2,240,000
1975	4,086,000,000	75,800,000	680,000
1980	4,454,000,000	73,600,000	-440,000
1985	4,850,000,000	79,200,000	1,120,000
1990	5,278,000,000	85,600,000	1,280,000
1995	5,687,000,000	81,800,000	-760,000

Questions 10-12

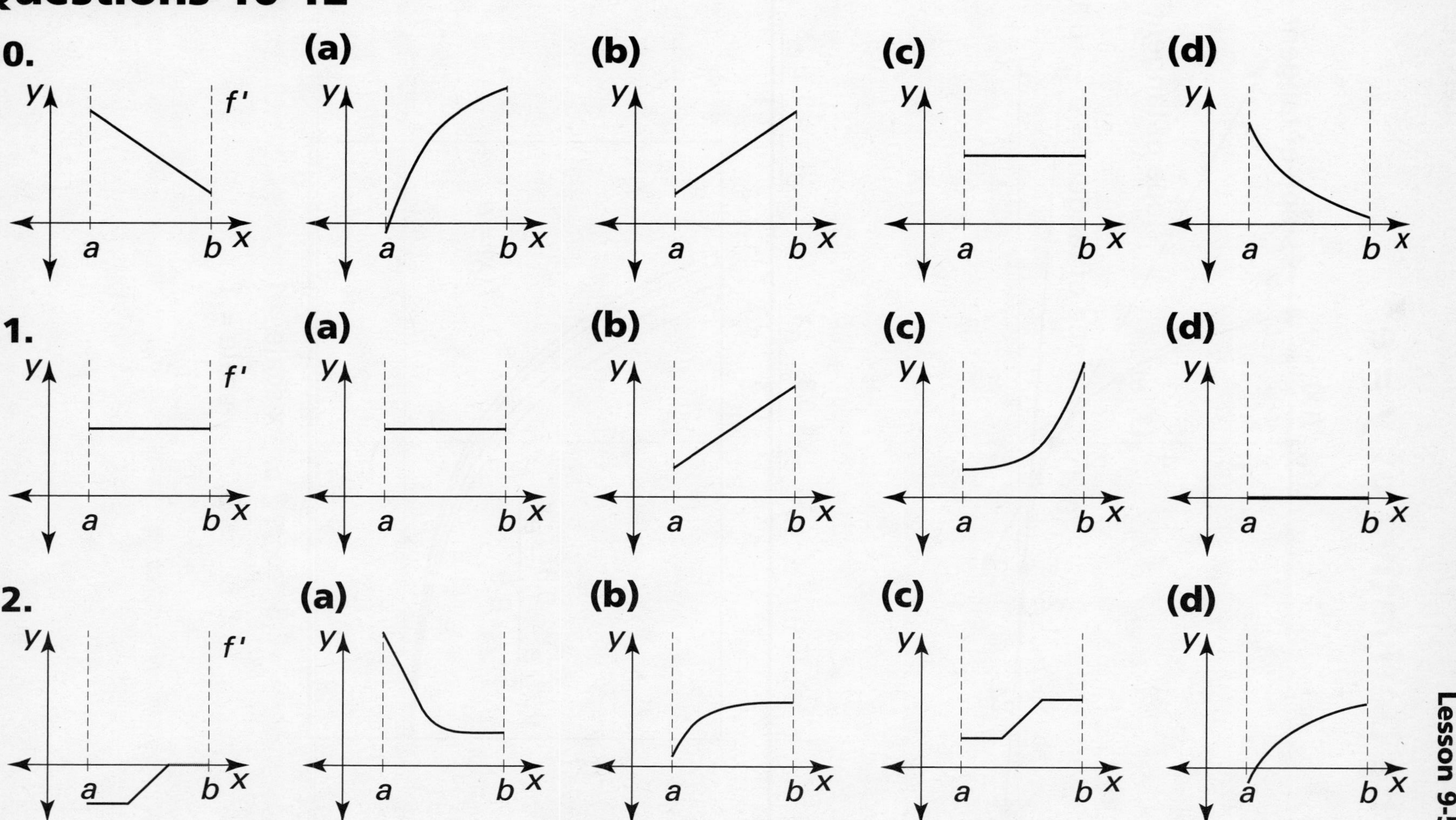

The Derivative of $y = e^x$

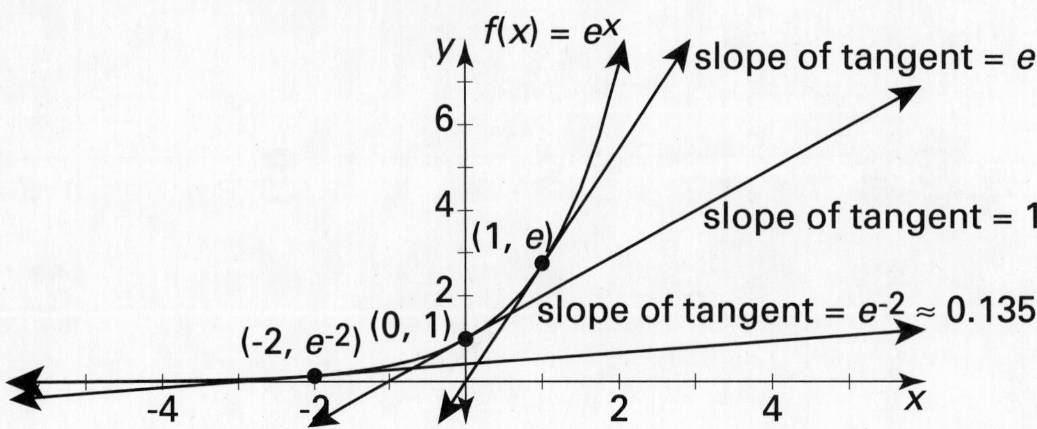

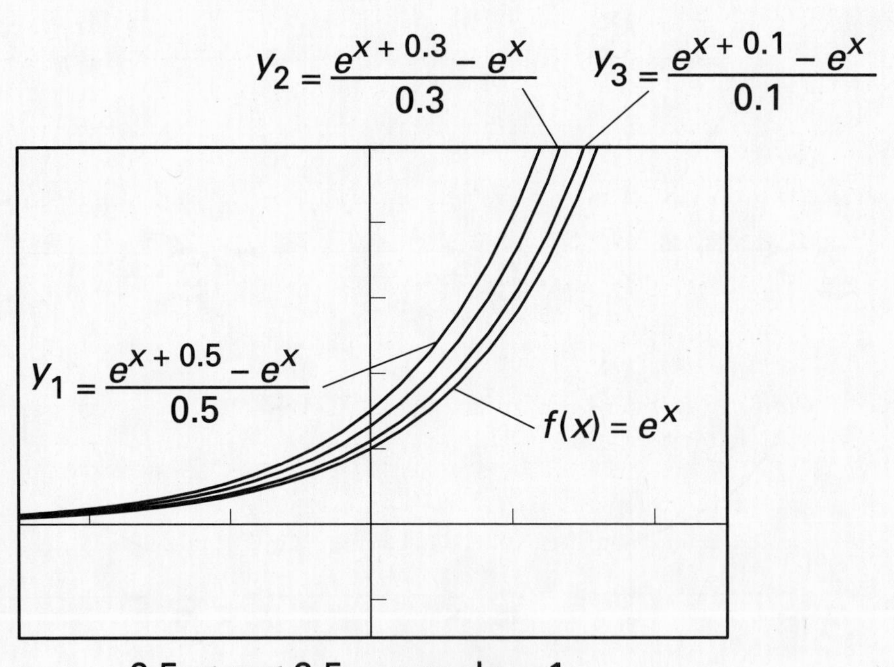

$-2.5 \le x \le 2.5$, x-scale = 1
$-1.5 \le y \le 5$, y-scale = 1

Warm-up

Lesson 10-1

Consider the symbols *A, B,* and *C.*

1. Write all sets of 3 symbols from *A, B, C,* without repetition.
2. Write all collections of 3 symbols from *A, B, C,* with repetition.
3. Write all strings of 3 symbols from *A, B, C,* without repetition.
4. Write all strings of 3 symbols from *A, B, C,* with repetition.

Warm-up

Lesson 10-2

Two teams *A* and *B* play each other until one of them loses twice.

1. Draw a tree diagram with all possibilities of this situation and indicate who wins with each possibility.
2. If the teams are evenly matched and team *A* loses the first game, what is the probability that it will win the match?

Warm-up

Lesson 10-3

Take a permutation of *k* of the four letters *a, e, s,* and *t*. For each value of *k* from 1 to 4, what is the probability that your permutation is a word in the English language?

Warm-up

Lesson 10-4

Consider all the subsets of the set {1, 2, 3, 4, 5}.

1. How many subsets have only even numbers as elements?
2. How many subsets have only odd numbers as elements?
3. How many subsets have both even numbers and odd numbers as elements?
4. How many subsets have neither even numbers nor odd numbers as elements?

Warm-up

Lesson 10-5

1. Expand $(3x - y)^4$.
2. Verify your answer to Question 1 by substituting 2 for x and 6 for y.

Warm-up

Lesson 10-6

Given that about 51% of the babies born in the United States are boys, and assuming that births of boys and girls are independent, what is the probability that in a family of three children, the eldest is a boy, the second is a girl, and the third is a boy?

Warm-up

Lesson 10-7

Work with a partner to compare your answers to the questions in the In-class Activity on page 639 in the Student Edition.

Warm-up

Lesson 10-8

1. According to the work in Lesson 10-7, how many terms are in the expansion of $(x + y + z)^4$?
2. $(x + y + z)^2 = x^2 + y^2 + z^2 + 2xy + 2xz + 2yz$. Square this six-term polynomial to obtain the full expansion of $(x + y + z)^4$.

Example 1

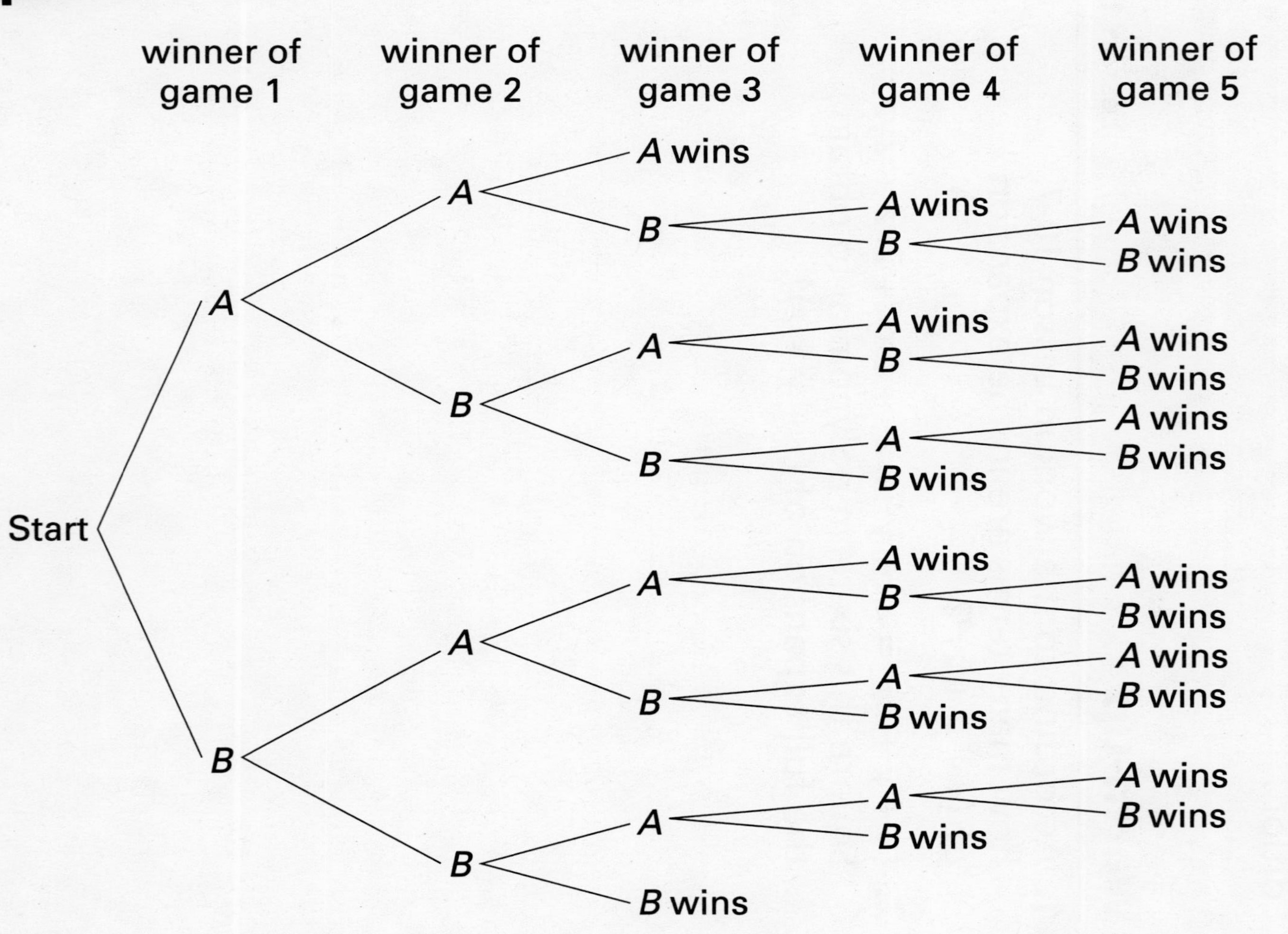
winner of game 1
winner of game 2
winner of game 3
winner of game 4
winner of game 5
Start
A
B
A wins
B wins
A wins
B wins
A wins
B wins
A wins
B wins
A wins
B wins
A wins
B wins
A wins
B wins
A wins
B wins
A wins
B wins
A wins
B wins

Pascal's Triangle

row 0 → 1

row 1 → 1 1

row 2 → 1 2 1

row 3 → 1 3 3 1

row 4 → 1 4 6 4 1

row 5 → 1 5 10 10 5 1

row 6 → 1 6 15 20 15 6 1

row 7 → 1 7 21 35 35 21 7 1

row 8 → 1 8 28 56 70 56 28 8 1

row 9 → 1 9 36 84 126 126 84 36 9 1

row 10 → 1 10 45 120 210 252 210 120 45 10 1

Question 11

$\binom{n}{r-1} + \binom{n}{r} = \dfrac{n!}{(r-1)(n-r+1)!} + \dfrac{n!}{r!(n-r)!}$	____________________
$= \dfrac{r \bullet n!}{r!(n-r+1)!} + \dfrac{n!(n-r+1)}{r!(n-r+1)!}$	____________________
$= \dfrac{[r + (n-r+1)]n!}{r!(n-r+1)!}$	____________________
$= \dfrac{(n+1)n!}{r!(n+1-r)!}$	Property of Opposites
$= \dfrac{(n+1)!}{r!(n+1-r)!}$	definition of __________
$= \binom{n+1}{r}$	____________________

Pascal's Triangle as a Triangle of Combinations

$$\binom{0}{0}$$
$$\binom{1}{0} \quad \binom{1}{1}$$
$$\binom{2}{0} \quad \binom{2}{1} \quad \binom{2}{2}$$
$$\binom{3}{0} \quad \binom{3}{1} \quad \binom{3}{2} \quad \binom{3}{3}$$
$$\binom{4}{0} \quad \binom{4}{1} \quad \binom{4}{2} \quad \binom{4}{3} \quad \binom{4}{4}$$
$$\vdots$$

$$1$$
$$1 \quad 1$$
$$1 \quad 2 \quad 1$$
$$1 \quad 3 \quad 3 \quad 1$$
$$1 \quad 4 \quad 6 \quad 4 \quad 1$$
$$\vdots$$

Warm-up

Lesson 11-1

Consider the cube below.

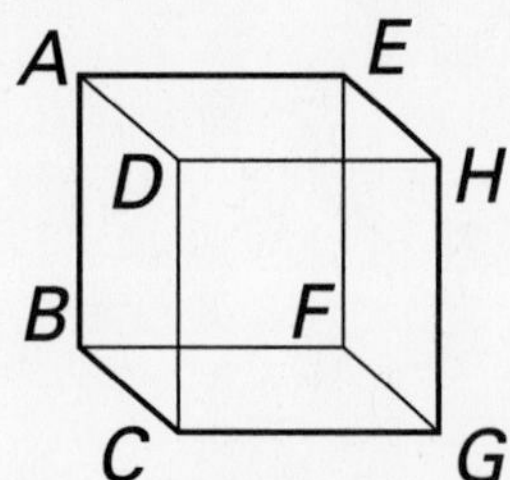

1. Is it possible to draw a path along the edges of the cube that contains each vertex exactly once and ends where it started? If so, draw such a path.
2. Is it possible to draw a path along its edges that contains each edge once and ends where it started? If so, draw such a path.

Warm-up

Lesson 11-2

Draw a graph with 5 vertices and the following number of edges.

1. 3 edges **2.** 5 edges **3.** 11 edges

Warm-up

Lesson 11-3

Eight people are at a party. Identify them as *A, B, C, D, E, F, G*, and *H*.

1. If each person says "Hello" to everyone else individually, how many "Hellos" will be spoken?
2. List them.

Warm-up

Lesson 11-4

In each case a polygon is identified. Consider the polygon and all its diagonals as a network, but do not consider intersections of diagonals as vertices in the network. Does the network have an Euler circuit?

1. Convex quadrilateral

2. Regular pentagon

3. Hexagon

4. Heptagon

Warm-up

Lesson 11-5

1. If $A = \begin{bmatrix} 1 & 2 \\ 3 & 4 \end{bmatrix}$, find A^4 by hand.

2. If you have technology that multiplies matrices, check your work using that technology.

Warm-up

Lesson 11-6

Let A be a 2×2 matrix in which the elements of the two rows are identical and the elements of each row sum to 1. Prove that $A^2 = A$.

Warm-up

Lesson 11-7

A regular octahedron can be formed by drawing two square pyramids with the same base whose faces are equilateral triangles. Draw such an octahedron and find the number of its vertices, edges, and faces.

Graphs of Euler and Hamilton

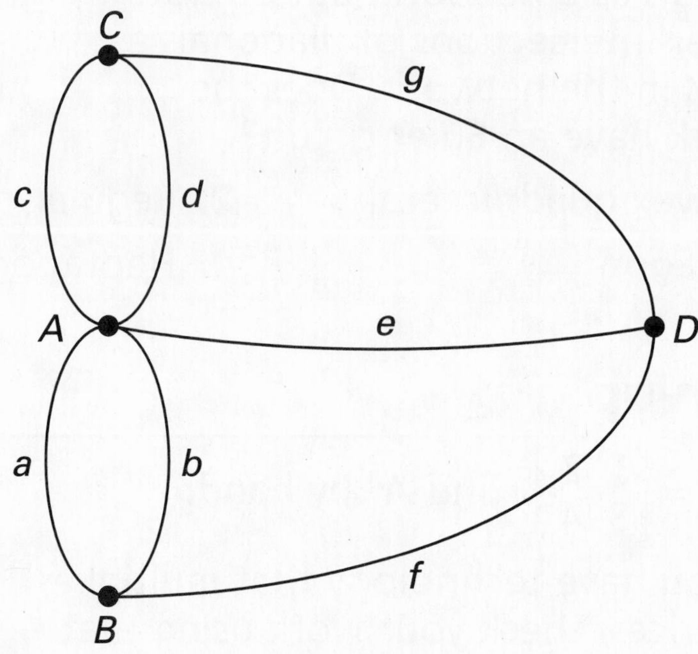

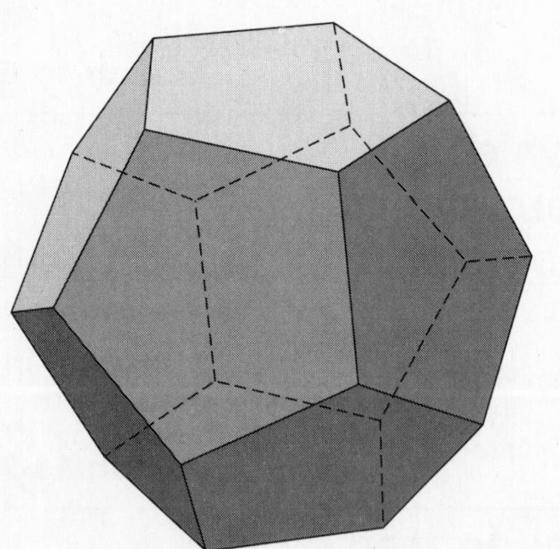

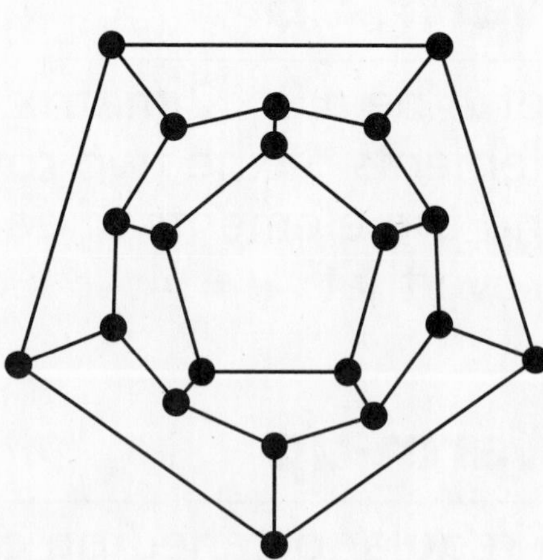

Example 2

Task		Time (days)	Prerequisite tasks
A	Preparing final house and site plans	3	none
B	Excavation and foundation construction	5	*A*
C	Framing and closing main structure	12	*B*
D	Plumbing	5	*C*
E	Wiring	3	*C*
F	Heating-cooling installation	7	*E*
G	Insulation and dry wall	9	*D, F*
H	Exterior siding, trim, and painting	15	*C*
I	Interior finishing and painting	7	*G*
J	Carpeting	3	*I*
K	Landscaping	4	*H*

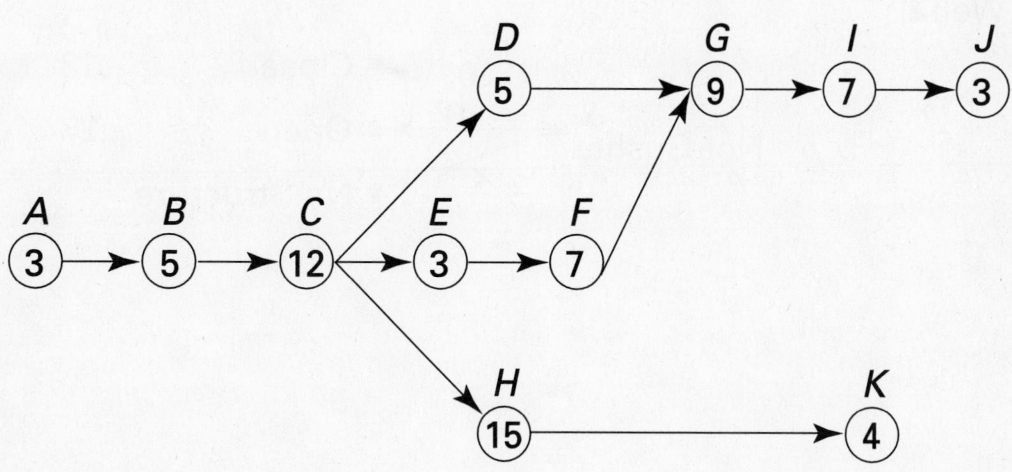

Example 3

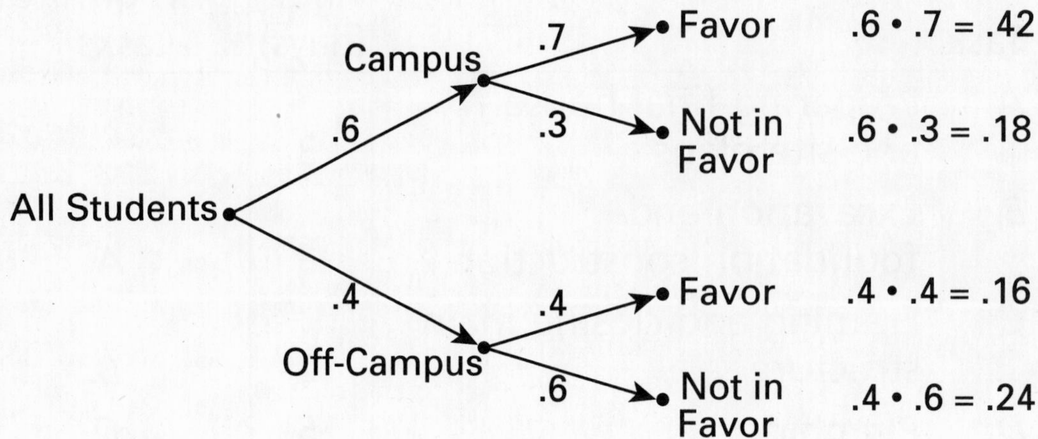

Question 13a

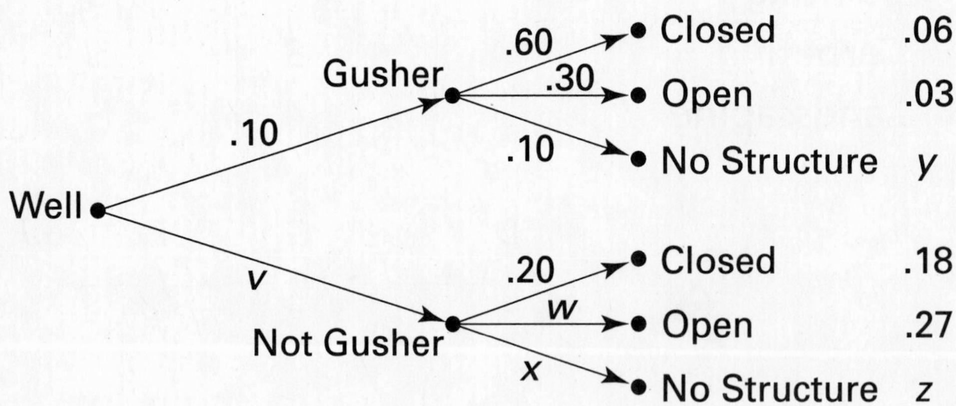

Additional Example 1

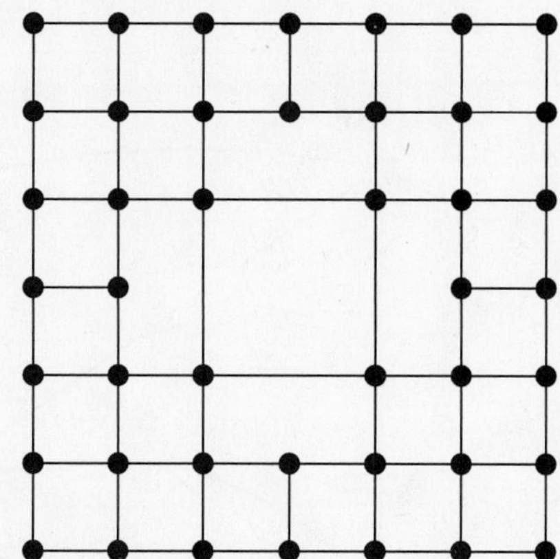

Additional Example 2

	Task	Time (month)
A	Choosing a project	1
B	Organizing a team	1
C	Obtaining funding	2
D	Setting up equipment	0.5
E	Running procedures	6
F	Keeping records	5.5
G	Writing a report	1

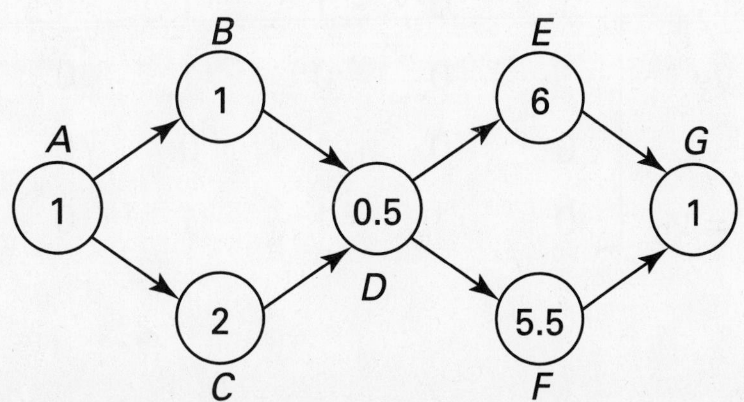

Example 3

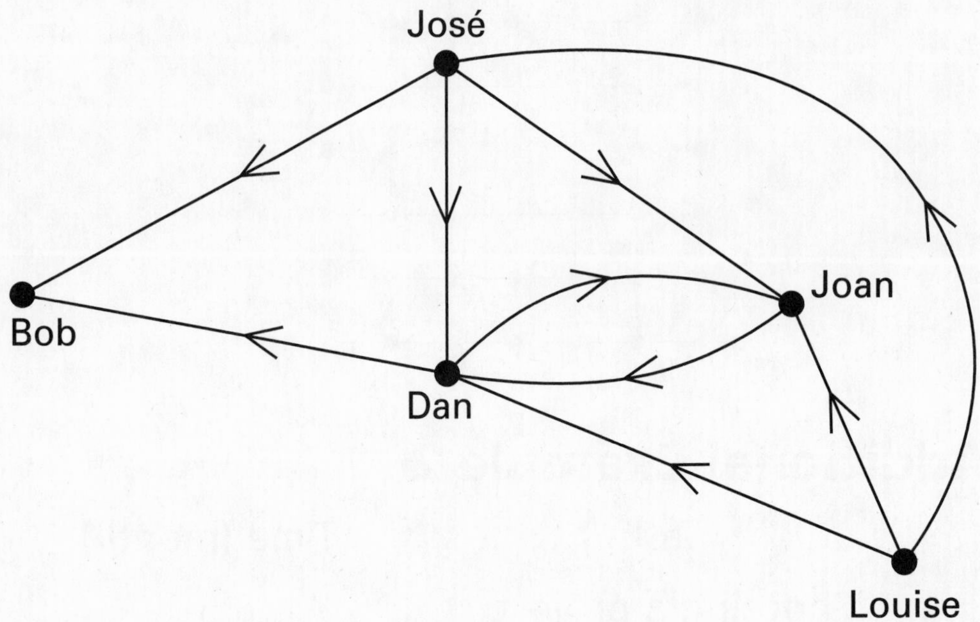

	Bob v_1	José v_2	Dan v_3	Joan v_4	Louise v_5
Bob = v_1	0	0	0	0	0
José = v_2	1	0	1	1	0
Dan = v_3	1	0	0	1	0
Joan = v_4	0	0	1	0	0
Louise = v_5	0	1	1	1	0

Example 4 and Questions 5 and 6

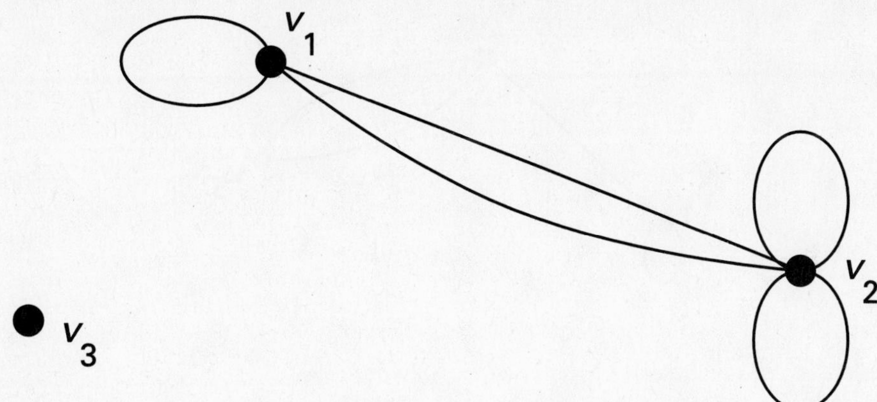

	v_1	v_2	v_3
v_1	1	2	0
v_2	2	2	0
v_3	0	0	0

5.

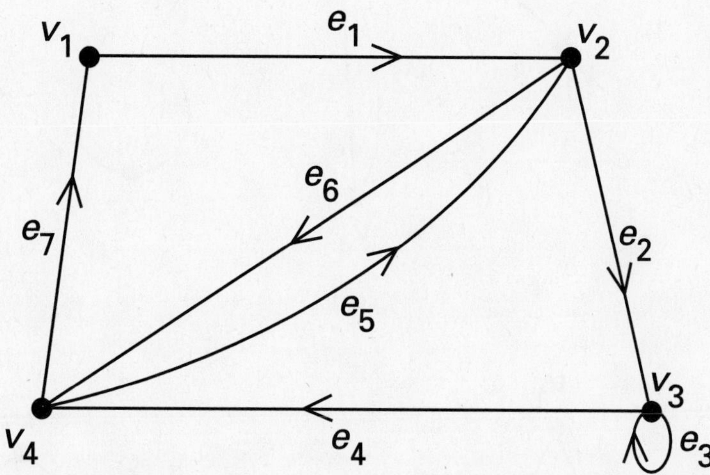

6.

$$\begin{bmatrix} 1 & 2 & 0 & 1 \\ 0 & 0 & 1 & 0 \\ 1 & 3 & 0 & 0 \\ 0 & 1 & 0 & 2 \end{bmatrix}$$

Questions 7, 10, 11, and 12

7.

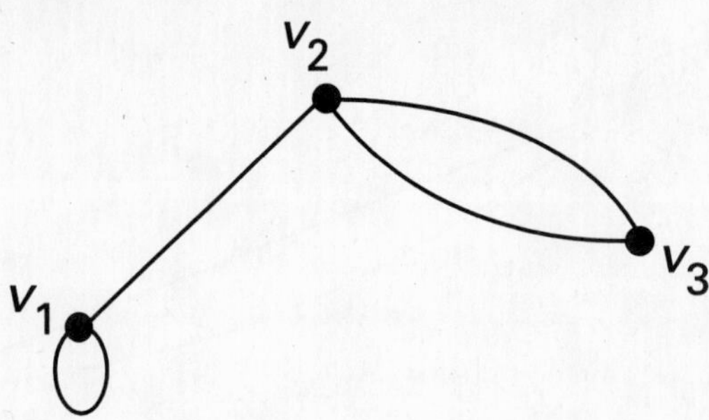

10.

$$\begin{bmatrix} 0 & 1 & 2 \\ 1 & 0 & 1 \\ 2 & 1 & 0 \end{bmatrix}$$

11.

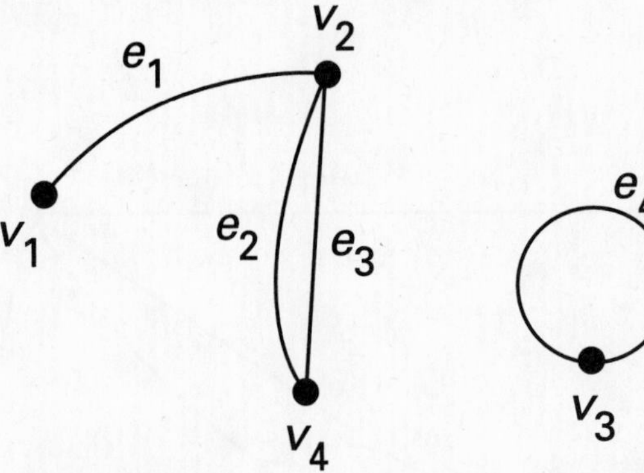

12.

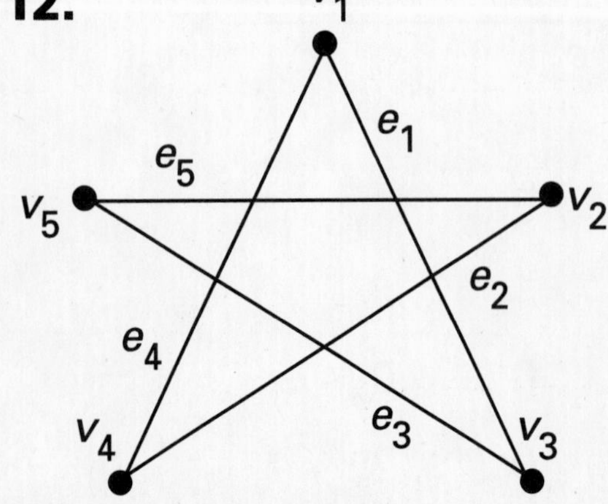

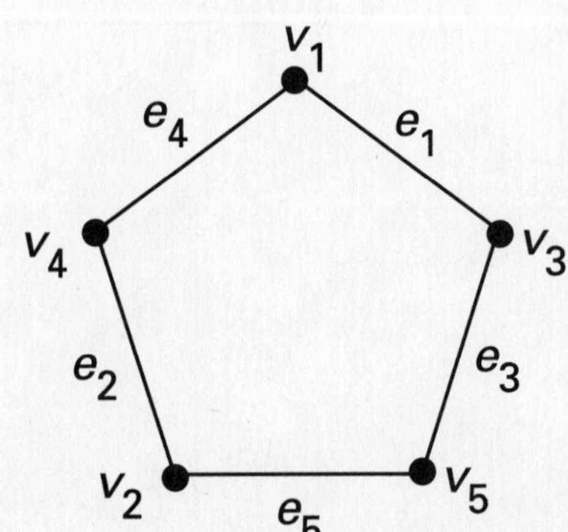

Questions 14, 15, and 17

14. vertices: $\{v_1, v_2, v_3, v_4\}$
edges: $\{e_1, e_2, e_3, e_4, e_5, e_6\}$
edge-endpoint function:

edge	endpoint
e_1	$\{v_1, v_2\}$
e_2	$\{v_1, v_3\}$
e_3	$\{v_3, v_1\}$
e_4	$\{v_3, v_3\}$
e_5	$\{v_2, v_4\}$
e_6	$\{v_3, v_4\}$

15.

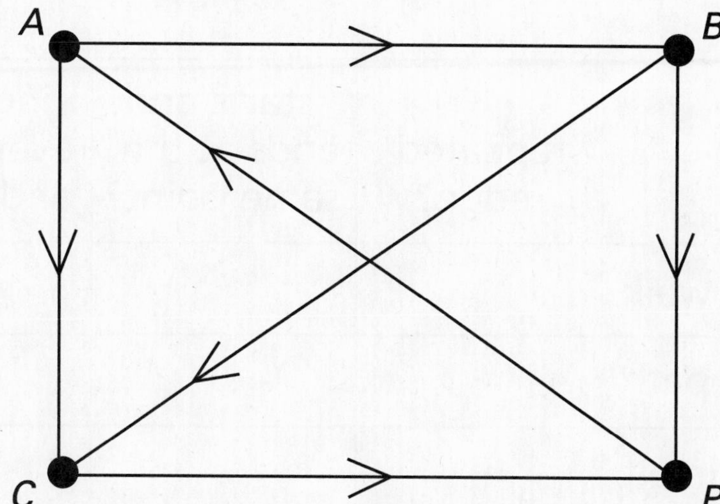

16.

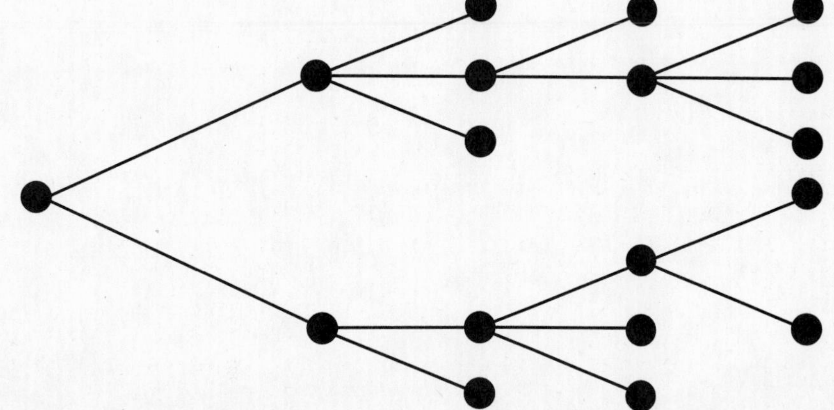

Graph *G* and Table

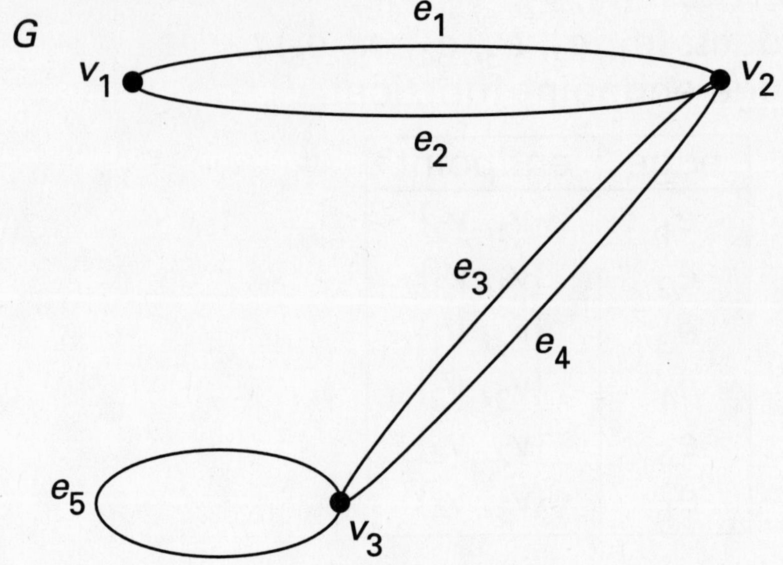

	repeated edge?	starts and ends at the same point?	includes every edge and vertex?
walk			
path			
circuit			
Eular circuit			

Questions 1, 2, and 4

1–2.

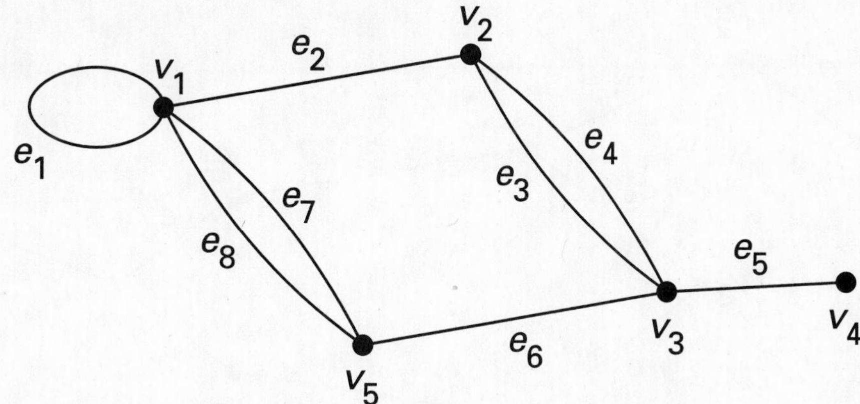

4. a.

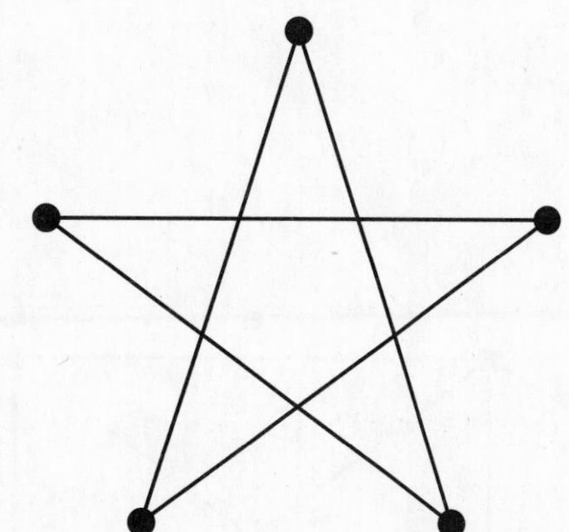

b.

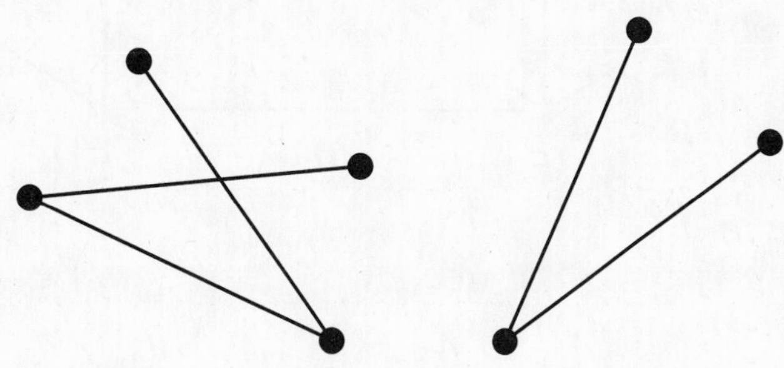

c.

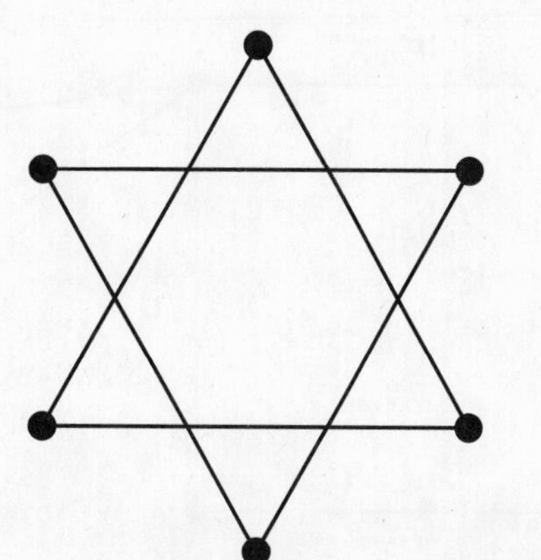

Questions 5, 6, and 7

5.

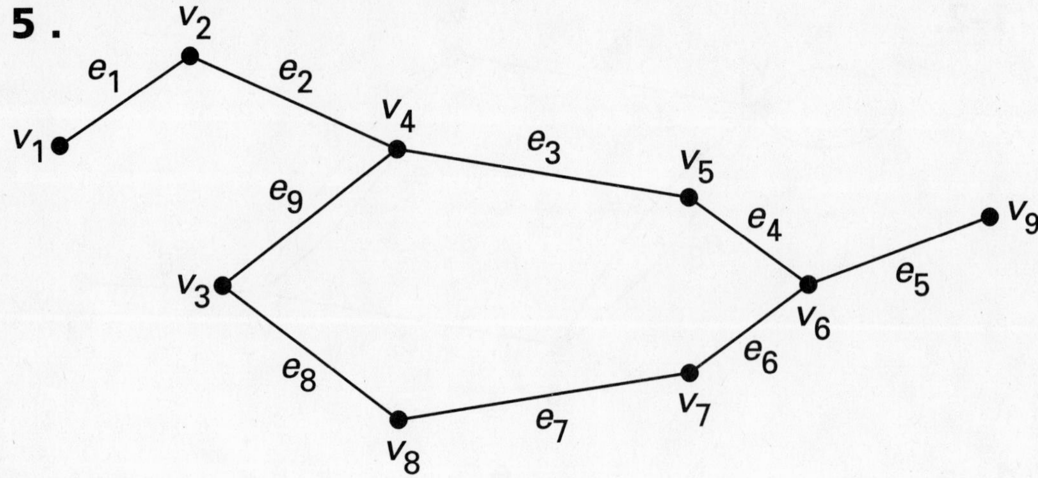

6.

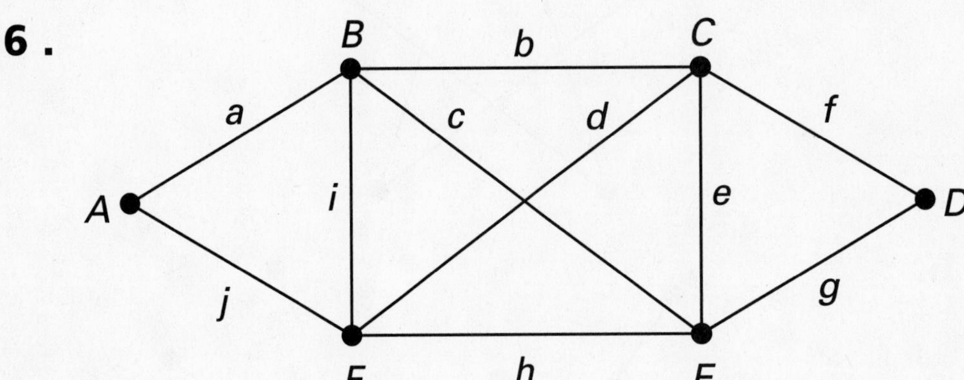

7.

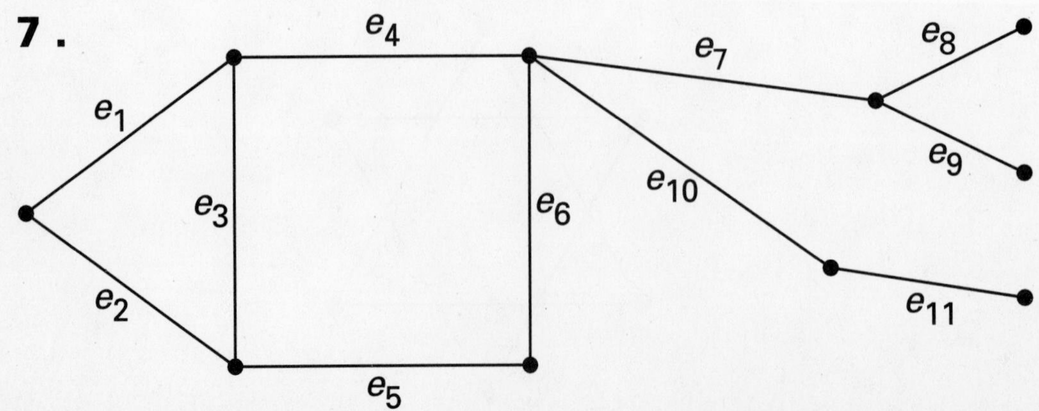

Question 8

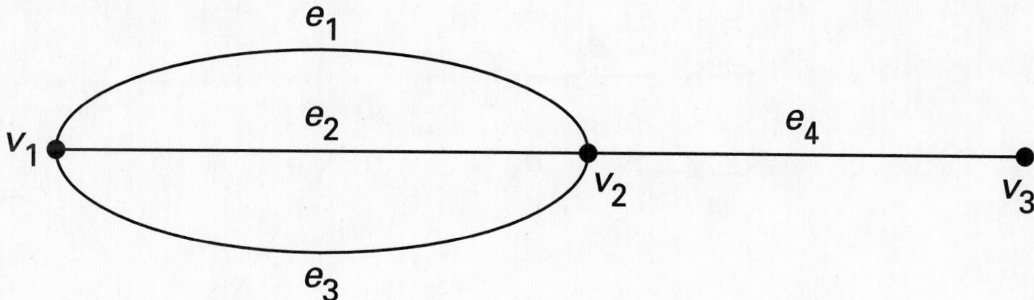

Question 12

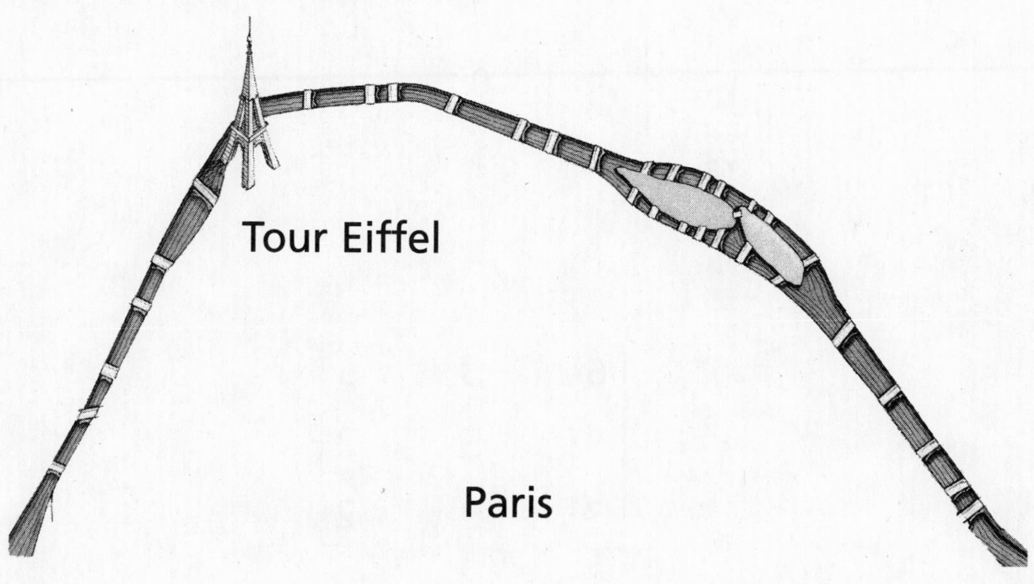

Example 1

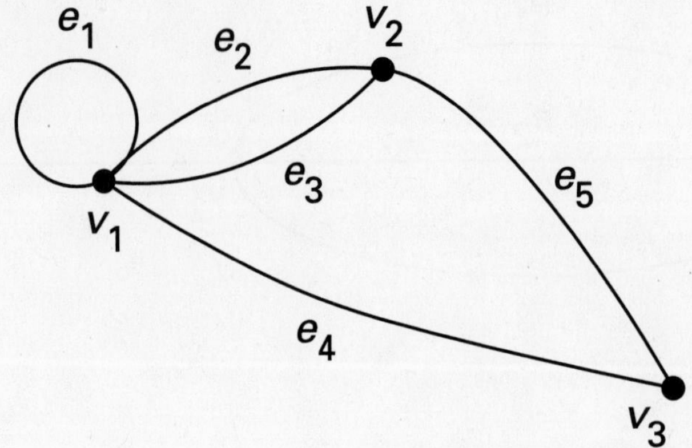

$$A = \begin{array}{c} \\ v_1 \\ v_2 \\ v_3 \end{array} \begin{array}{c} \begin{array}{ccc} v_1 & v_2 & v_3 \end{array} \\ \begin{bmatrix} 1 & 2 & 1 \\ 2 & 0 & 1 \\ 1 & 1 & 0 \end{bmatrix} \end{array}$$

$$A^2 = \begin{bmatrix} 6 & 3 & 3 \\ 3 & 5 & 2 \\ 3 & 2 & 2 \end{bmatrix}$$

Questions 2, 9, and 12

2.

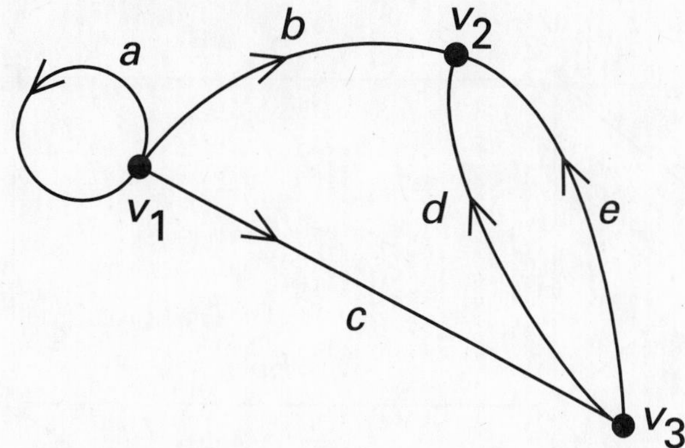

9.

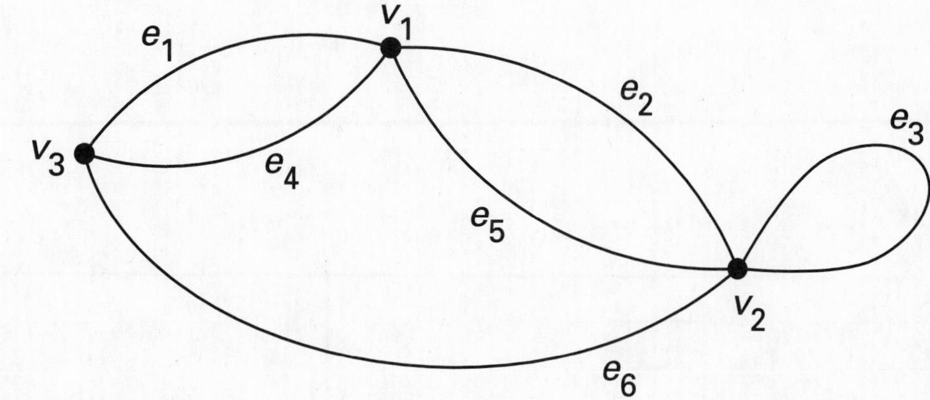

12.

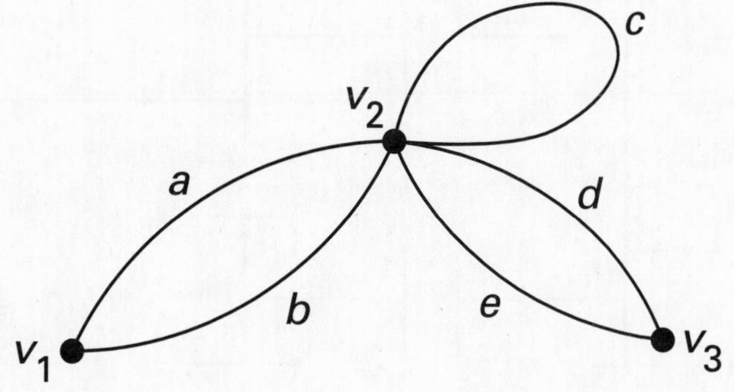

Questions 15 and 16

15.

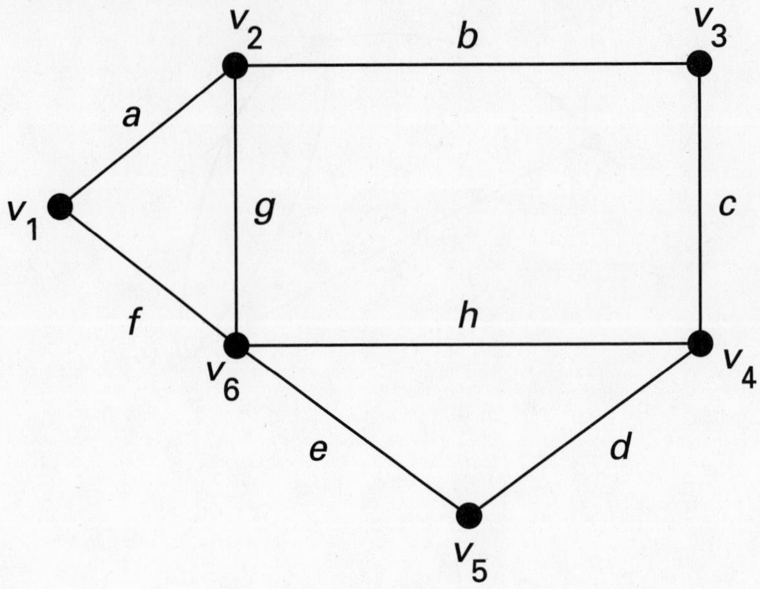

16.

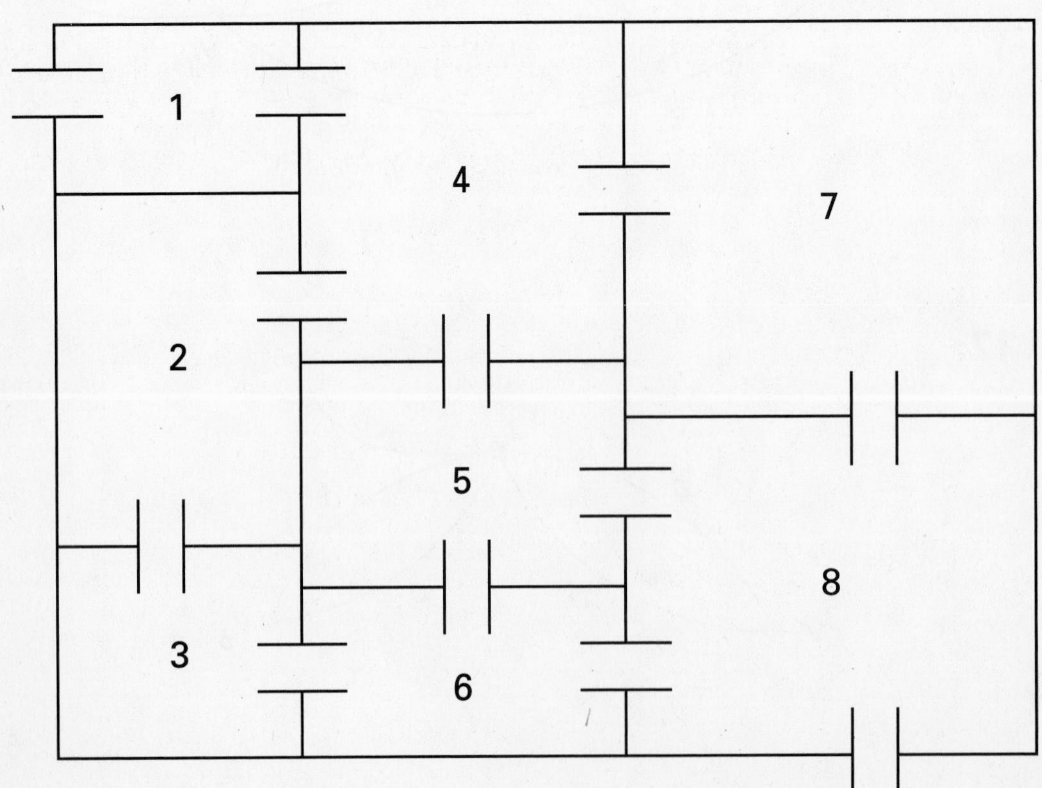

Questions 18 and 21

18.

	v_1	v_2	v_3	v_4
v_1	0	1	2	3
v_2	1	0	1	2
v_3	2	1	0	1
v_4	3	2	1	0

21.

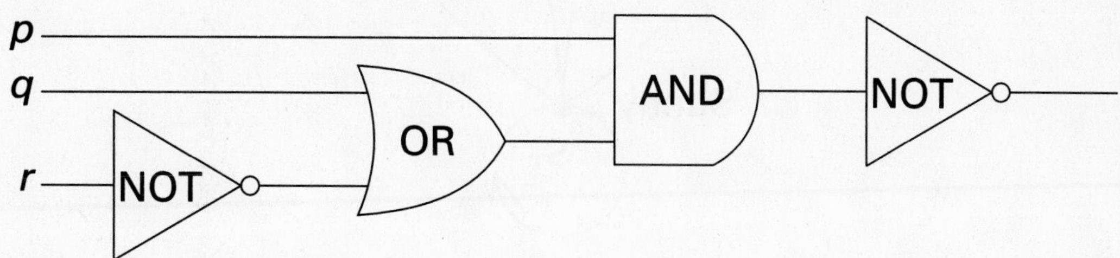

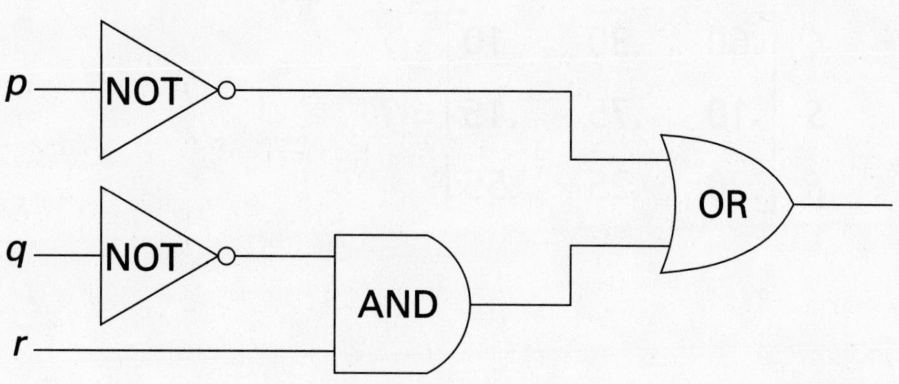

Graph and Matrix T

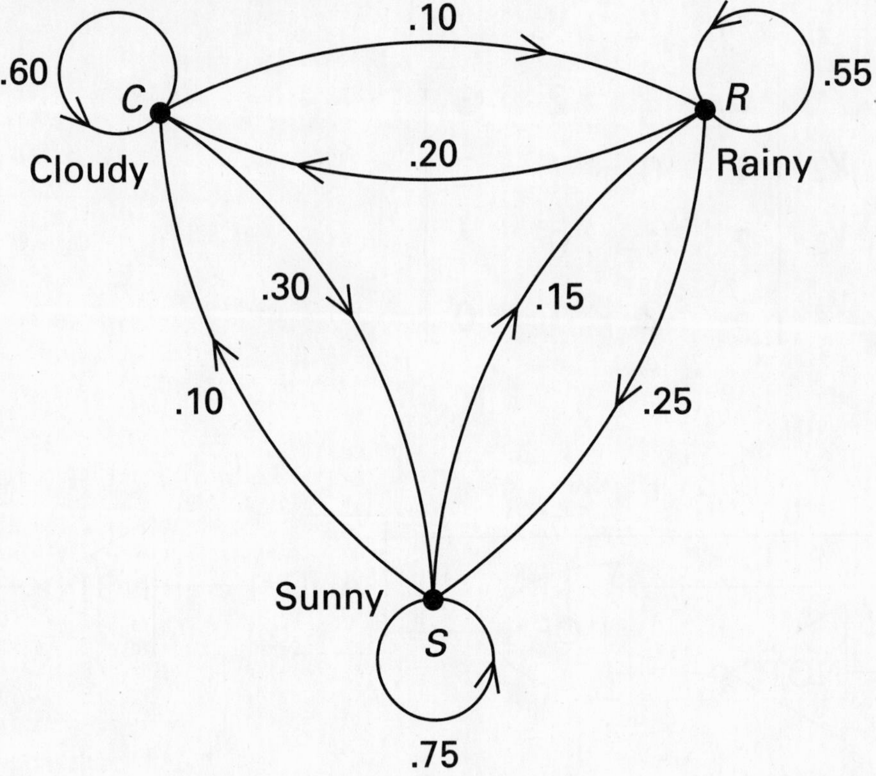

$$
\begin{array}{c} \\ C \\ S \\ R \end{array}
\begin{array}{c} \begin{array}{ccc} C & S & R \end{array} \\ \begin{bmatrix} .60 & .30 & .10 \\ .10 & .75 & .15 \\ .20 & .25 & .55 \end{bmatrix} \end{array} = T
$$

Questions 14–16

14.

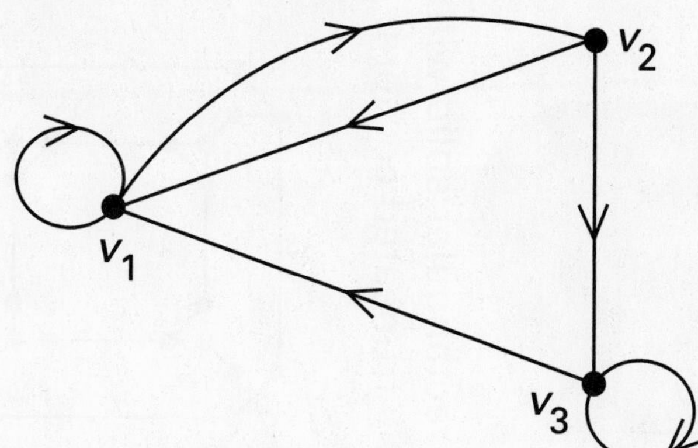

15.

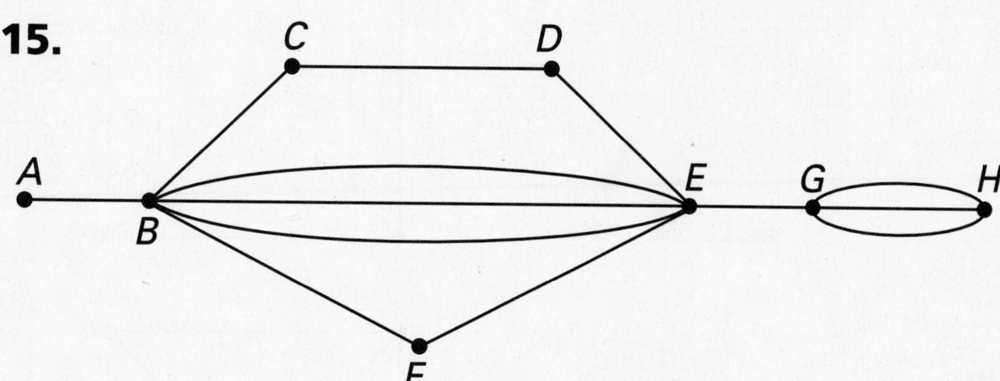

16.

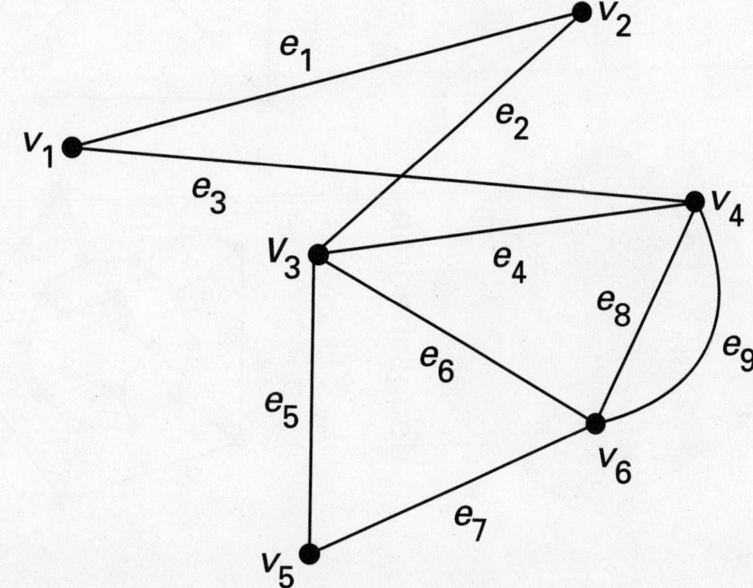

Polyhedra and their Graphs

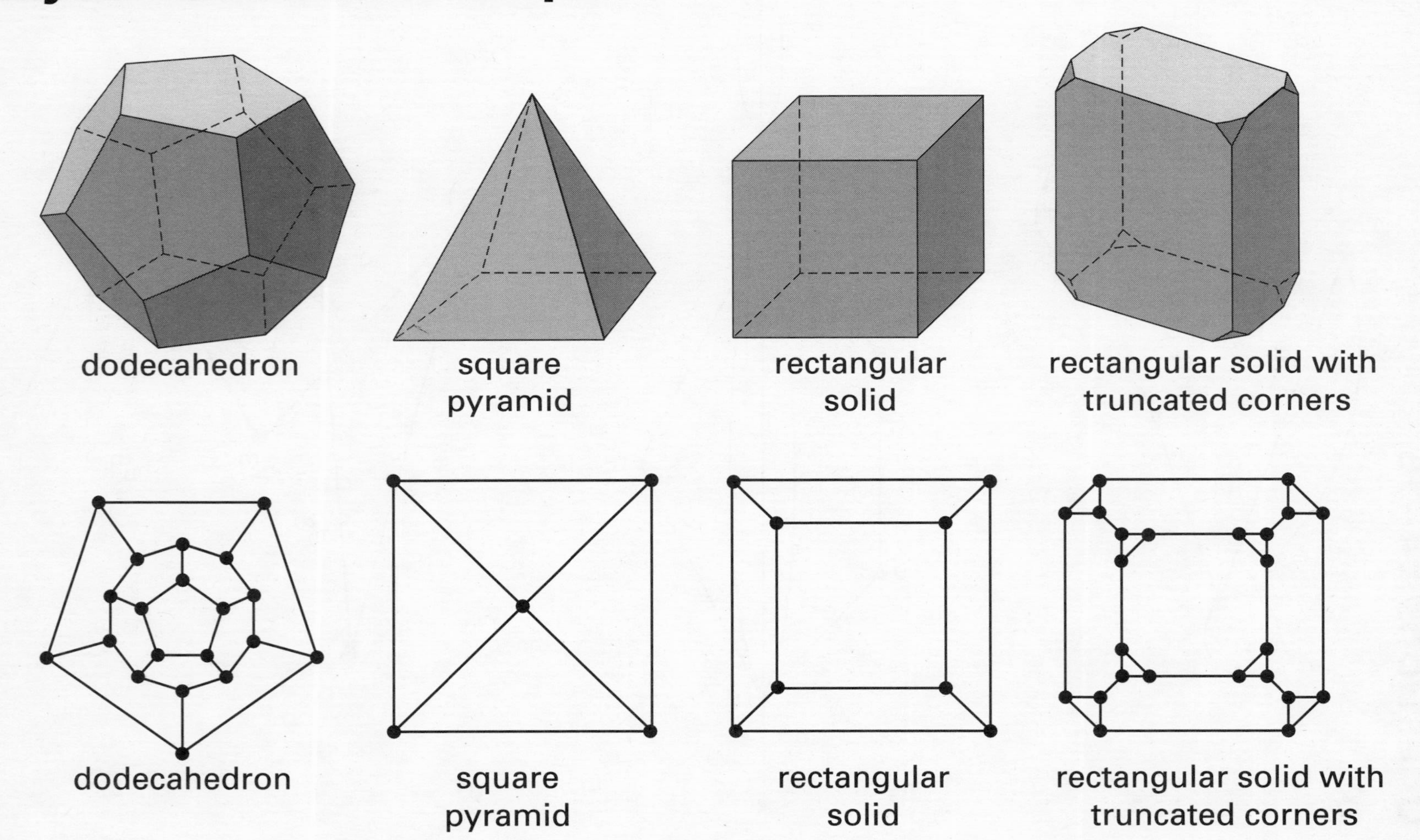

Questions 5–8, 11, 12, and 17

5.

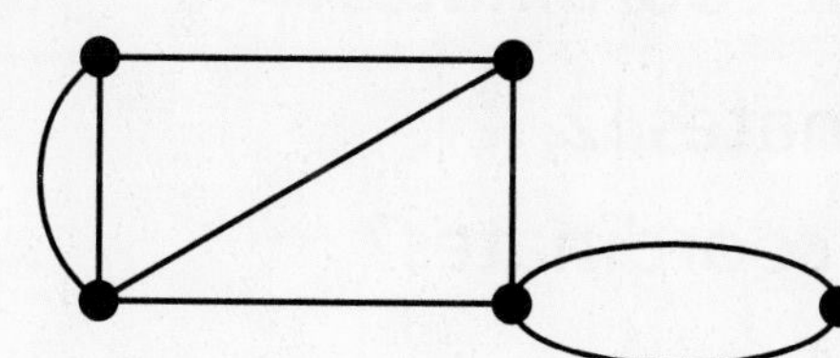

6.

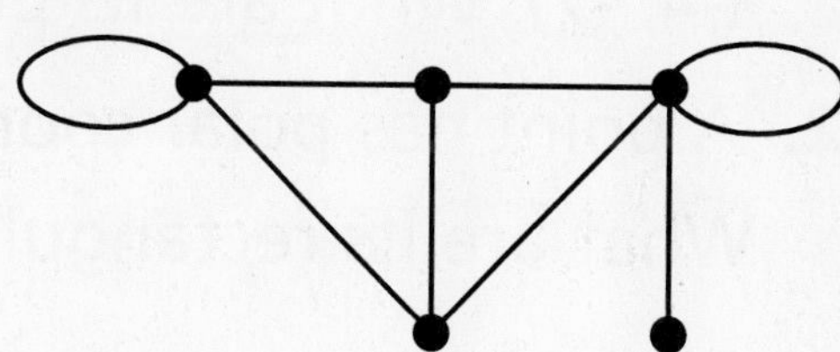

7.

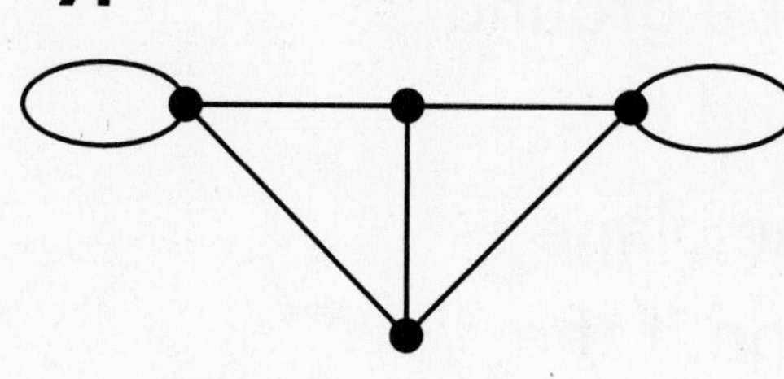

8.

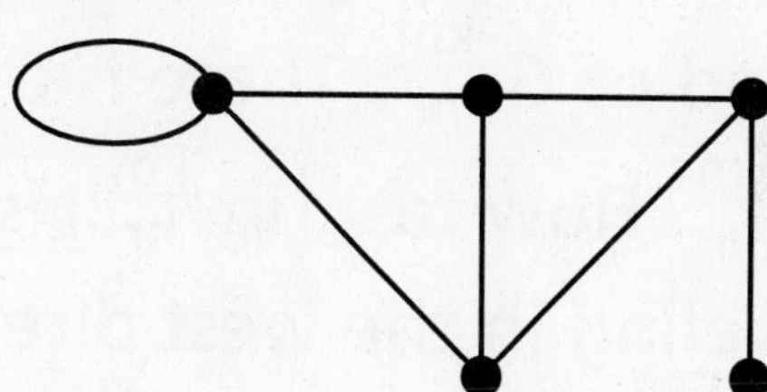

11.

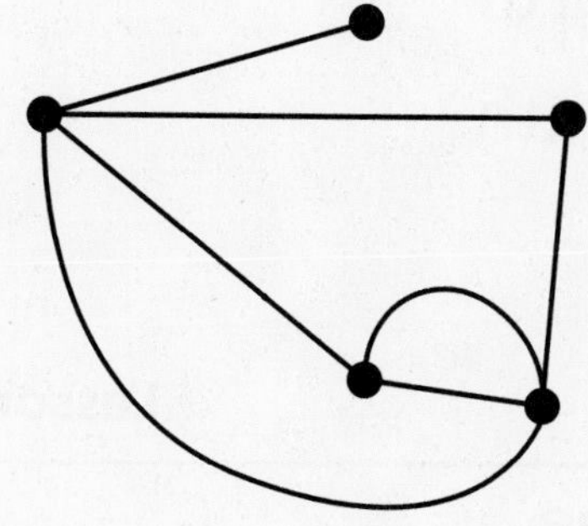

12.

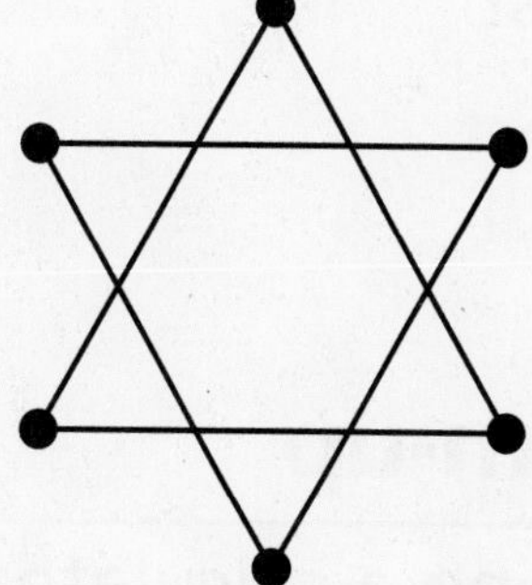

17.

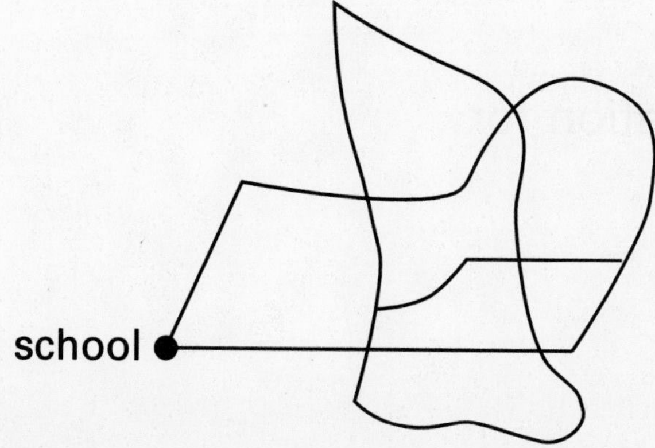

Warm-up

Lesson 12-1

1. A point has rectangular coordinates (-4, -7). What are its polar coordinates?
2. A point has polar coordinates $\left[2, \frac{\pi}{5}\right]$. What are its rectangular coordinates?

Warm-up

Lesson 12-2

A plane is going due west at a ground speed of $G\,\frac{\text{km}}{\text{hr}}$. There is a wind of $W\,\frac{\text{km}}{\text{hr}}$. How fast $\left(\text{in } \frac{\text{km}}{\text{hr}}\right)$ is the plane traveling in the west direction if the wind is coming from the following directions?

1. east
2. north
3. west
4. south

Warm-up

Lesson 12-3

1. Using a calculator, graph the parametric equations
$$\begin{cases} x = 2 + 3t \\ y = 5 - t \end{cases}$$
2. Give an x-y equation for the graph.

Warm-up

Lesson 12-4

Let * be an operation on ordered pairs of real numbers, defined as follows: $(a, b) * (c, d) = ac + bd$.

1. Is * commutative?

2. Is the set of ordered pairs of real numbers closed under *?

3. Is * associative?

Warm-up

Lesson 12-5

A trunk is one meter long, 45 centimeters wide, and 28 centimeters high in its internal dimensions. To the nearest centimeter, what is the length of the longest inflexible thin rod that can fit inside this trunk?

Warm-up

Lesson 12-6

Find the area of the parallelogram with consecutive vertices (2, 10), (0, 0), and (4, 1).

Warm-up

Lesson 12-7

Refer to the diagram.

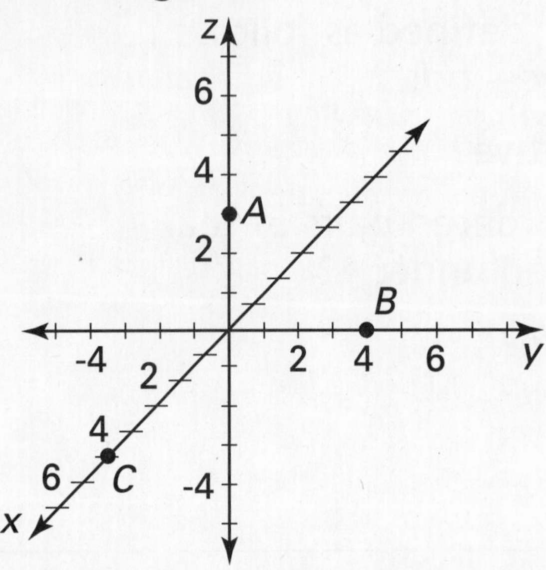

1. What are the coordinates of points *A, B,* and *C*?
2. How many lines contain points *A* and *B*? Points *A* and *C*? Points *B* and *C*?
3. How many planes contain points *A, B,* and *C*?

Warm-up

Lesson 12-8

Moe, Curly, and Shemp Howard were brothers and played the roles of the stooges in the "Three Stooges" movies. Curly was born 6 years after Moe and 8 years after Shemp. The sum of their years of birth was 5695. To find the years of their births, write a system of three linear equations and solve it.

Definitions and Basic Theorems About Vectors

Definition
A **vector** is a quantity that can be characterized by its direction and its magnitude.

Definition
The **polar representation** of a two-dimensional vector $\vec{v}$ with non-negative **magnitude** r and **direction** θ measured from the polar axis is $[r, \theta]$.

Definition
The **component representation** of a plane vector $\vec{u}$ is the ordered pair (u_1, u_2), the rectangular coordinates of the point at the top of the standard position arrow for u. The numbers u_1 and u_2 are the ***x*-component** and ***y*-component** of u, respectively, or the **horizontal** and **vertical components** of u.

Theorem
If $\vec{u} = (u_1 , u_2)$, then
$$|\vec{u}| = \sqrt{u_1^2 + u_2^2}.$$

Theorem
For all plane vectors $\vec{u}$ with direction θ,
$$\left[\, |\vec{u}|, \theta \,\right] = \left(|\vec{u}| \cos\theta, |\vec{u}| \sin\theta \right).$$

Example and Definition of Vector Addition

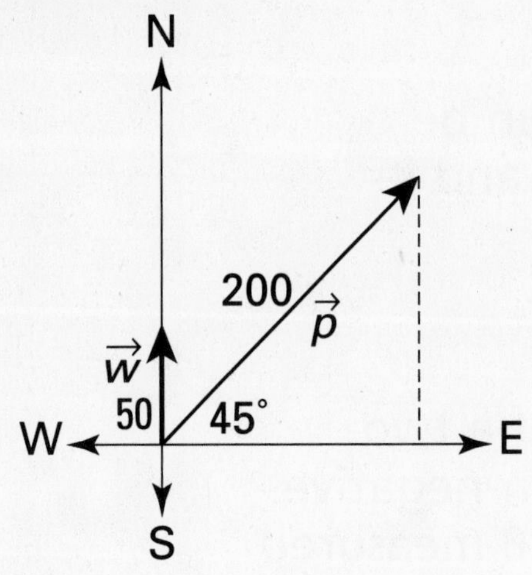

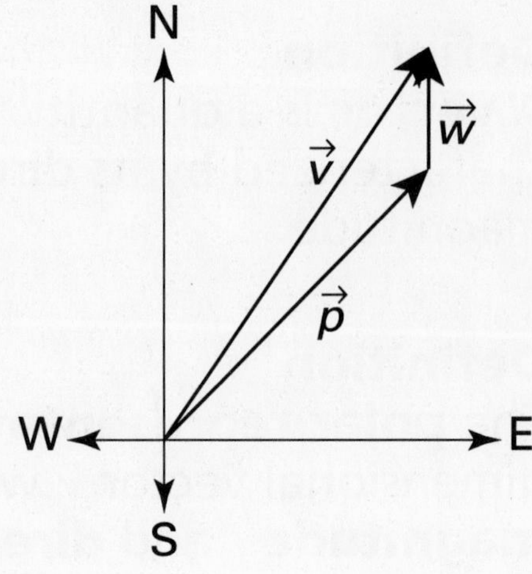

Definition

If $\vec{u} = (u_1, u_2)$ and $\vec{v} = (v_1, v_2)$, then the **sum of $\vec{u}$ and $\vec{v}$** written $\vec{u} + \vec{v}$, is the vector $(u_1 + v_1, u_2 + v_2)$.

Example 1

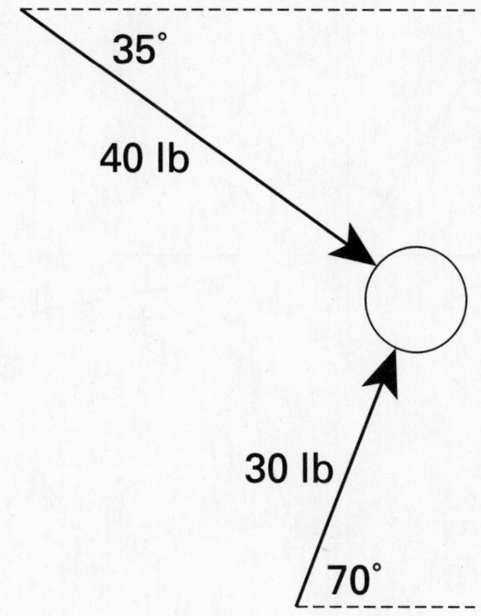

Example 2

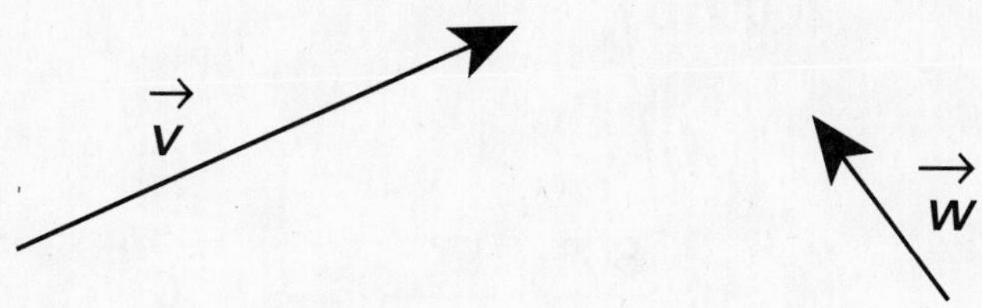

Questions 4, 6, and 15

4.

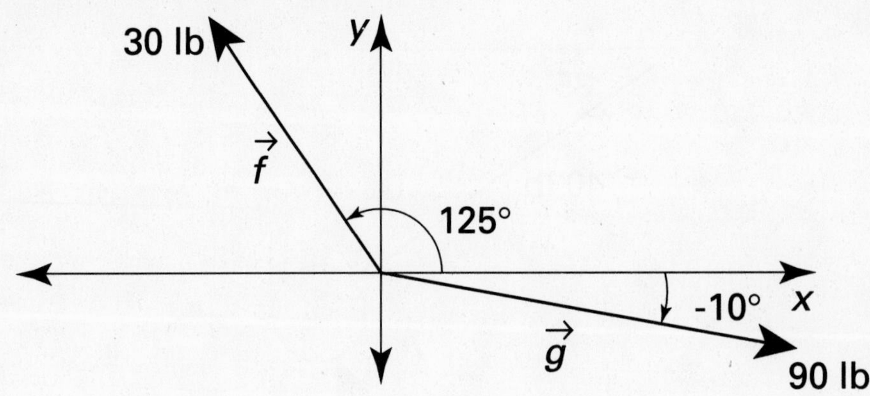

6.

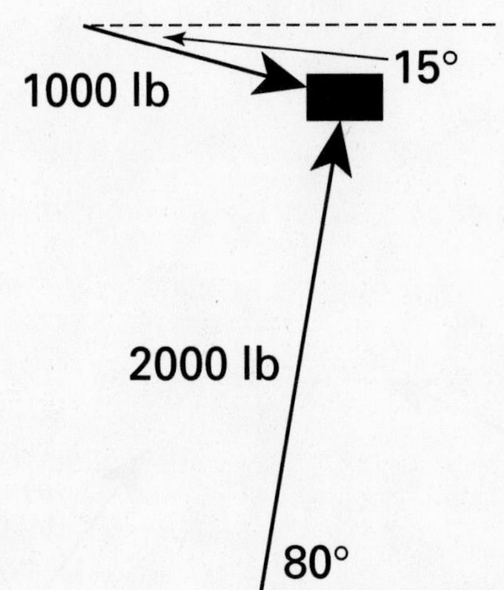

15.

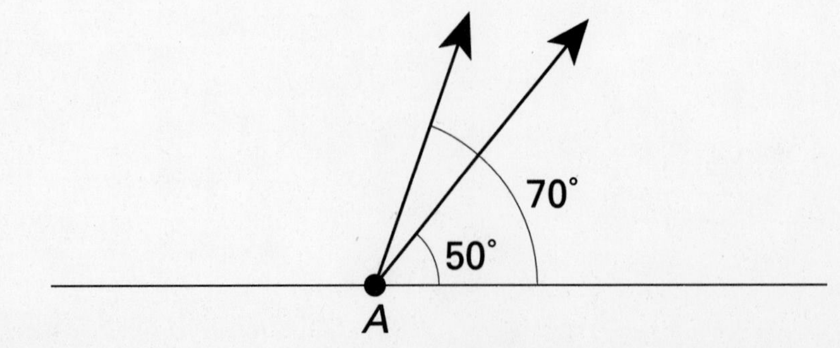

Vector and Parametric Equations for Lines

Theorem

A point $Q = (x, y)$ is on the line through $P = (x_0, y_0)$ parallel to the vector $\vec{v} = (v_1, v_2)$ if and only if there is a real number t with $\overrightarrow{PQ} = t\vec{v}$, or $(x - x_0, y - y_0) = t(v_1, v_2)$.

Theorem

The line through (x_0, y_0) that is parallel to the vector $\vec{v} = (v_1, v_2)$ has parametric equations

$$\begin{cases} x = x_0 + tv_1 \\ y = y_0 + tv_2, \end{cases}$$

where t may be any real number.

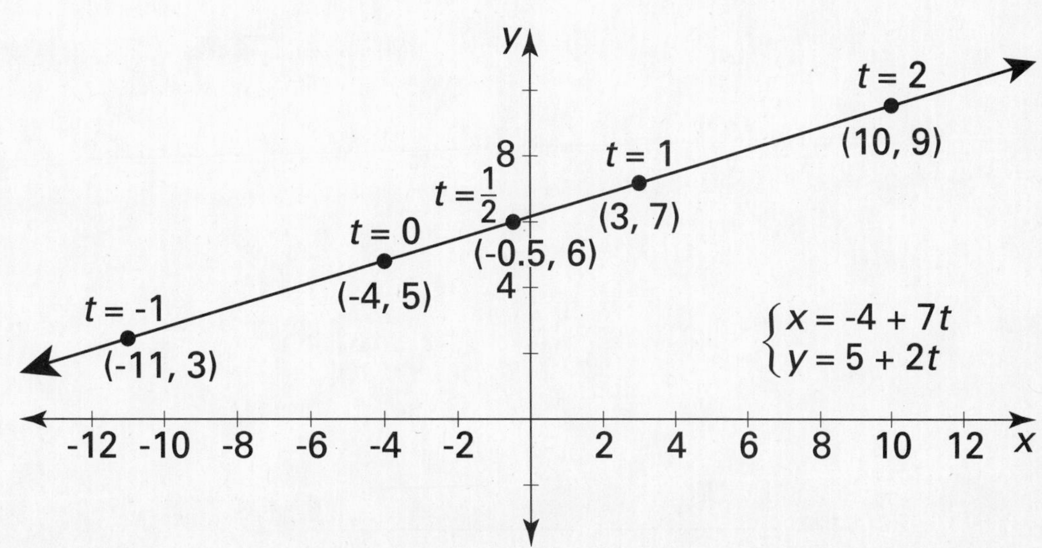

Example 1

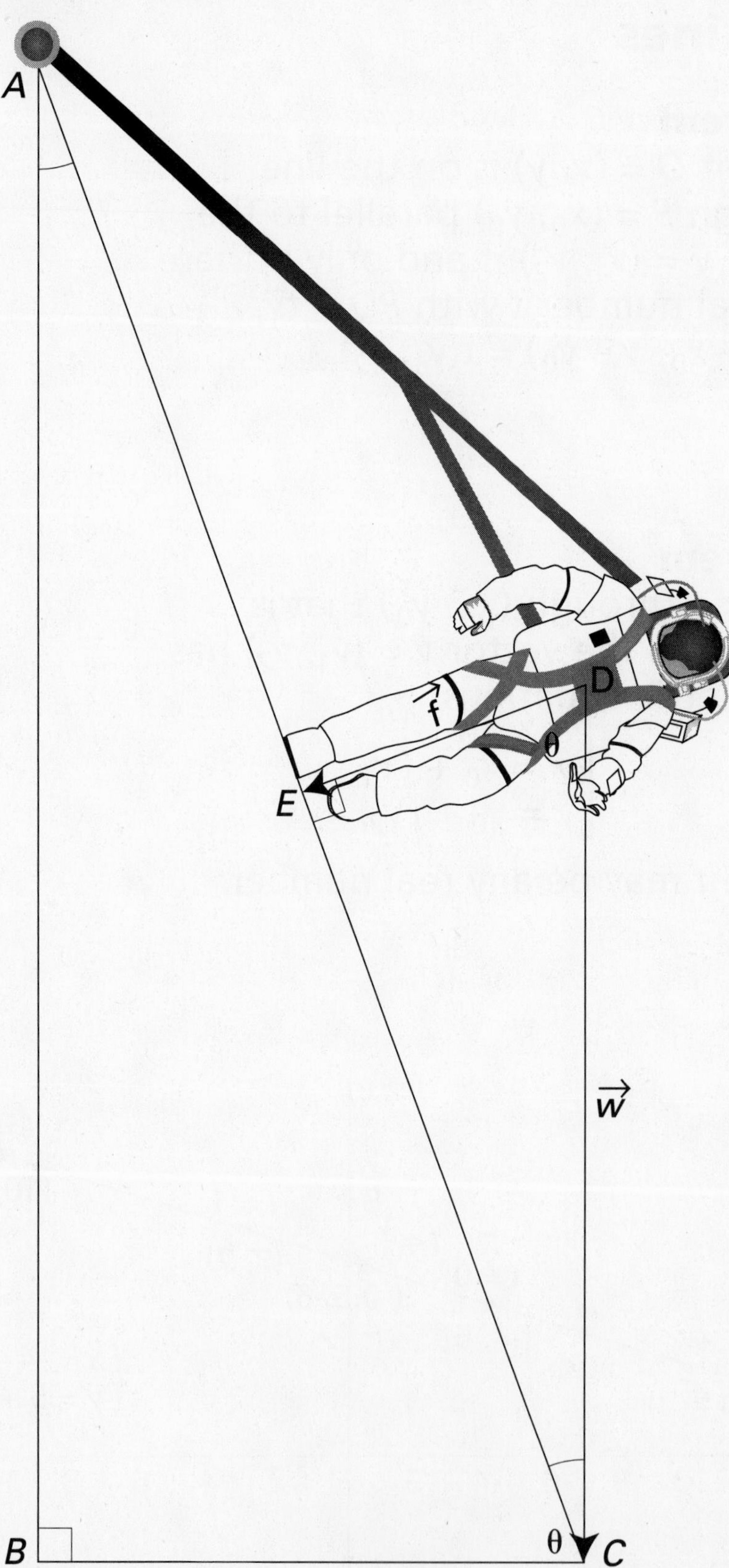

3-Dimensional Coordinate System

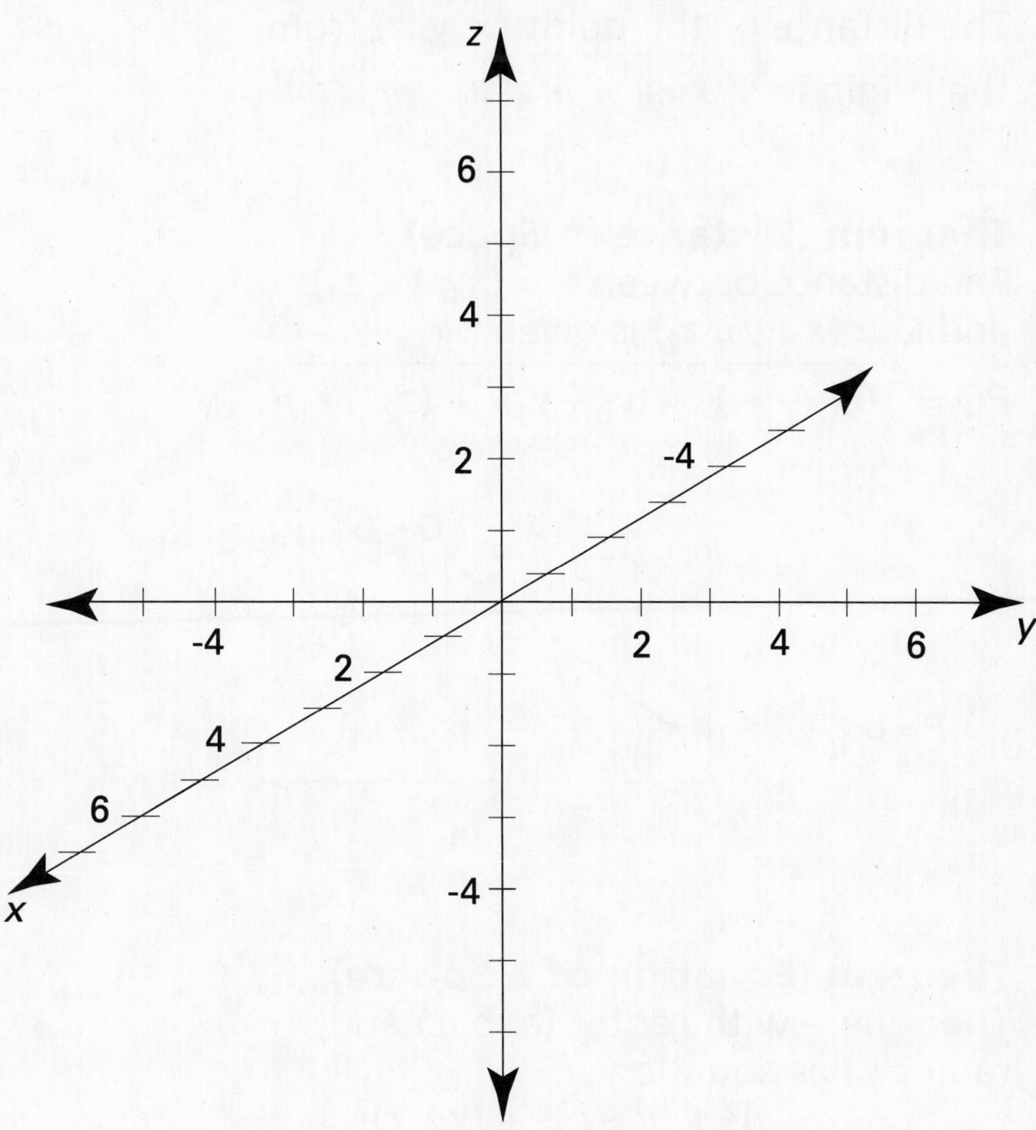

Theorems of the Lesson

Theorems
The distance of the point (x, y, z) from the origin is $\sqrt{x^2 + y^2 + z^2}$.

Theorem (Distance in Space)
The distance between $P = (x_1, y_1, z_1)$ and $Q = (x_2, y_2, z_2)$ is given by
$PQ = \sqrt{(x_2 - x_1)^2 + (y_2 - y_1)^2 + (z_2 - z_1)^2}$.

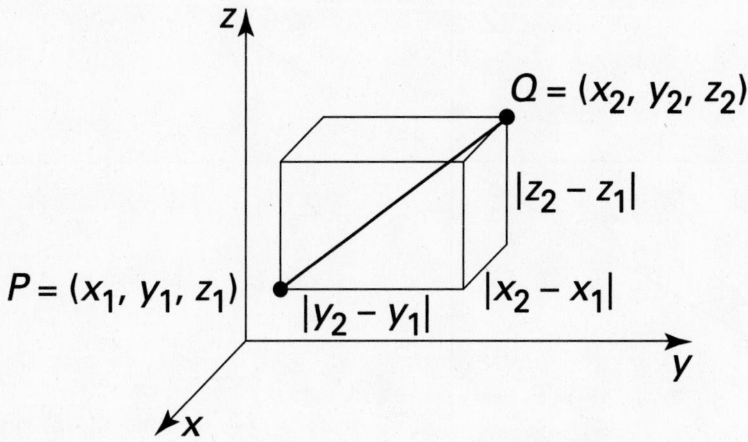

Theorem (Equation of a Sphere)
The sphere with center (a, b, c) and radius r has equation
$$r^2 = (x - a)^2 + (y - b)^2 + (z - c)^2.$$

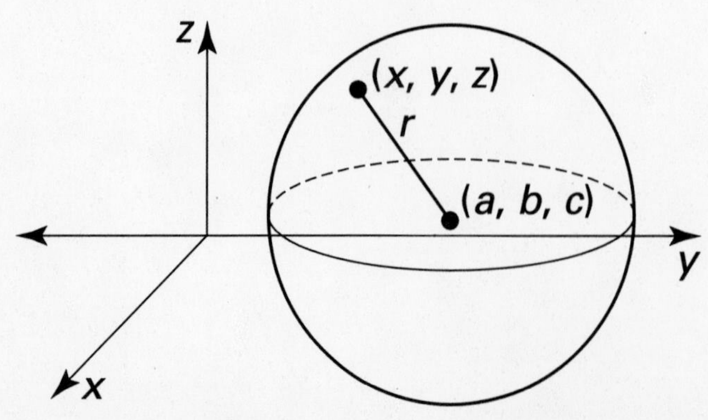

Example 2

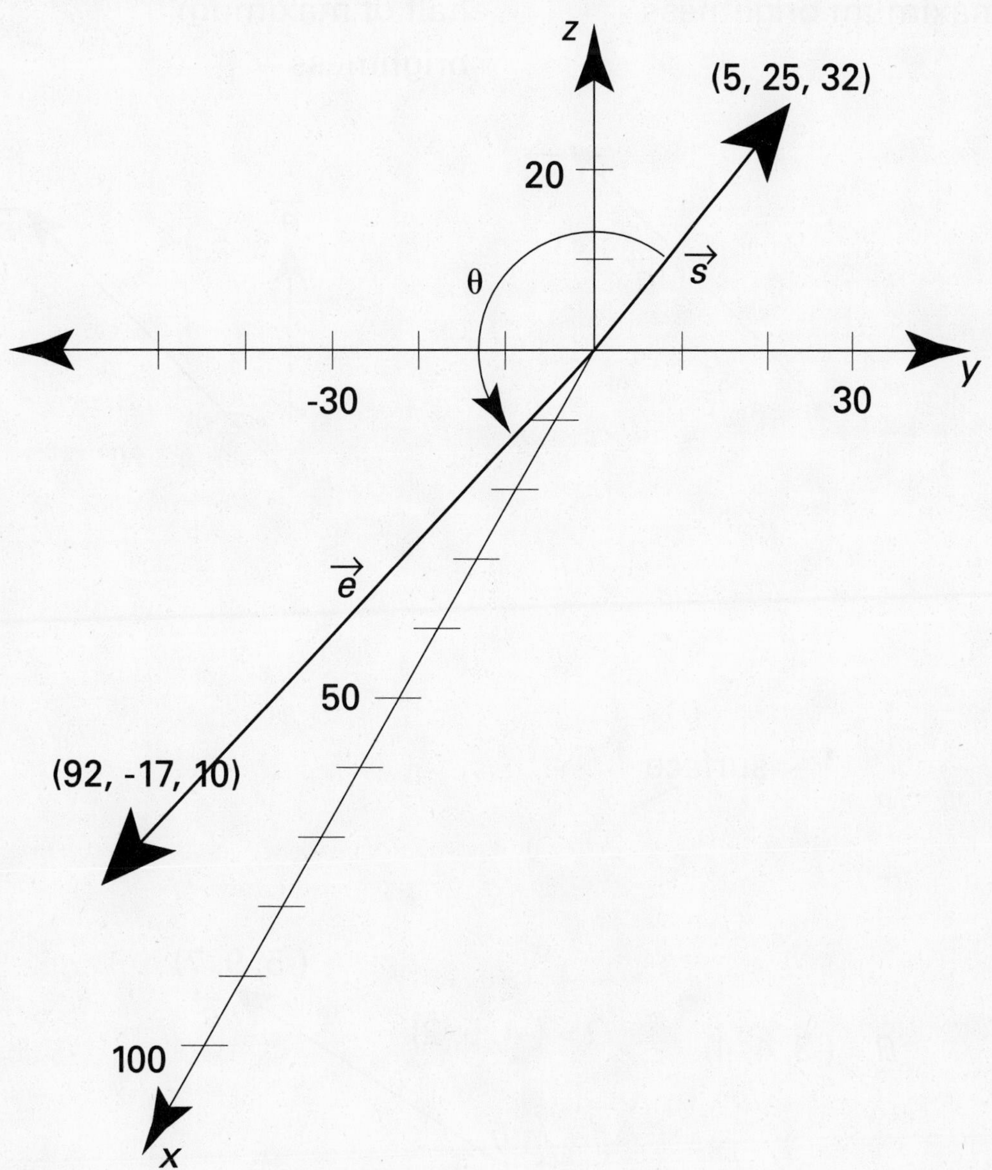

Question 19

$\theta = 0°$, $\cos\theta = 1$
maximum brightness

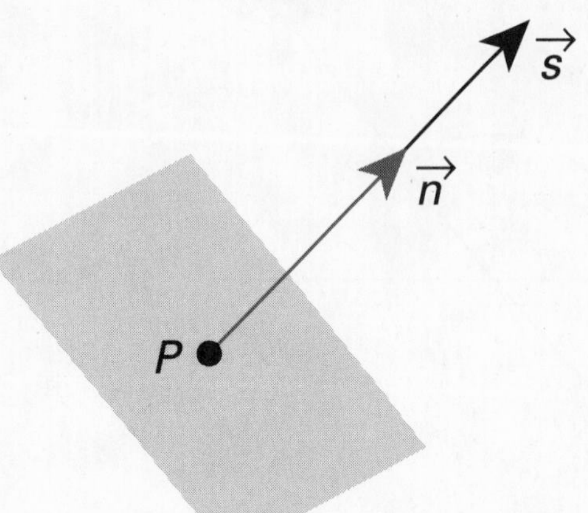

$\cos\theta = .5$
half of maximum brightness

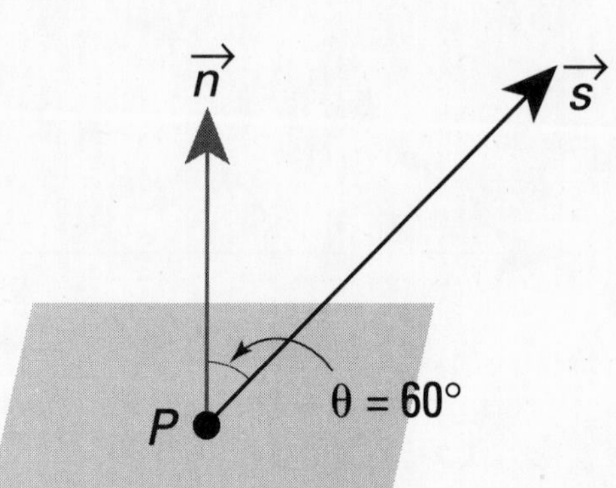

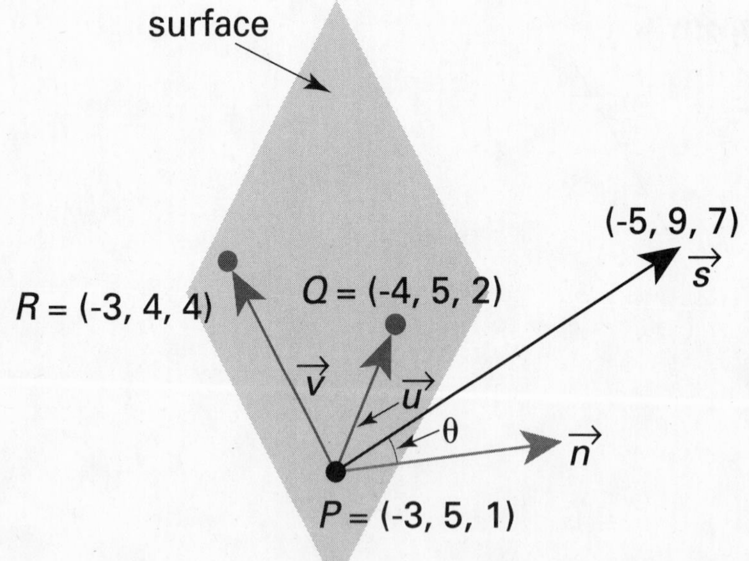

Example 1

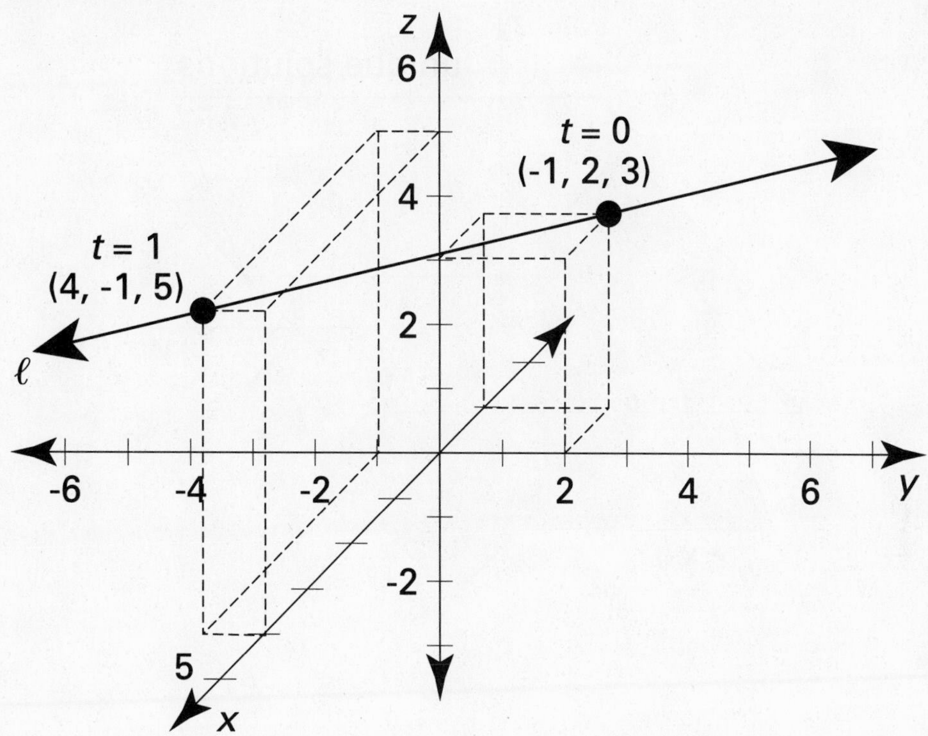

Example 2

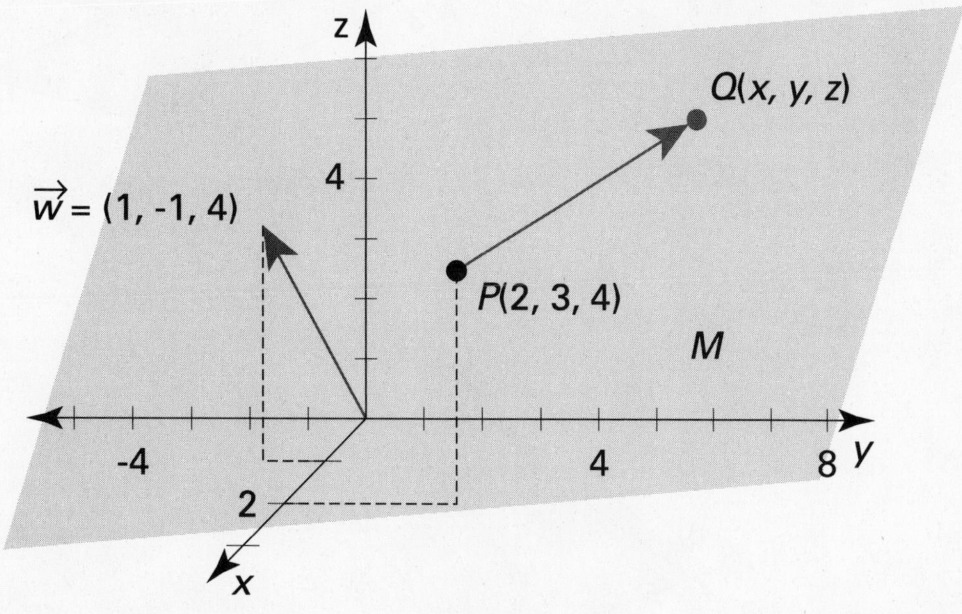

Various Intersections of Three Planes

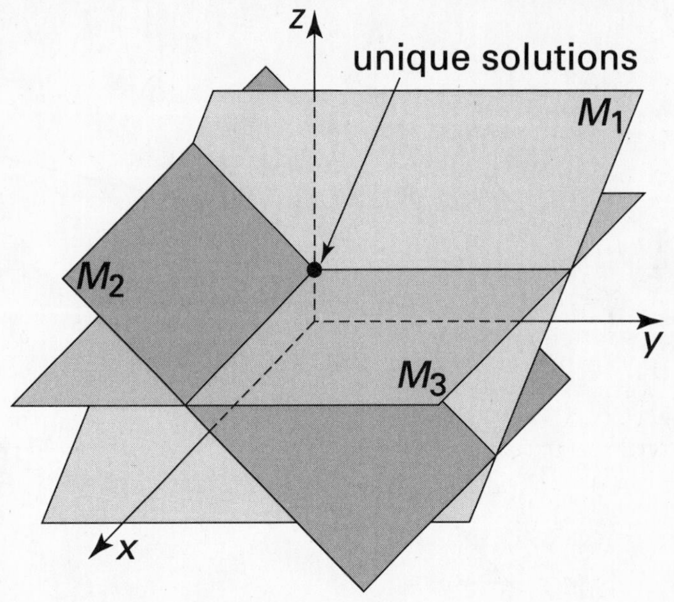

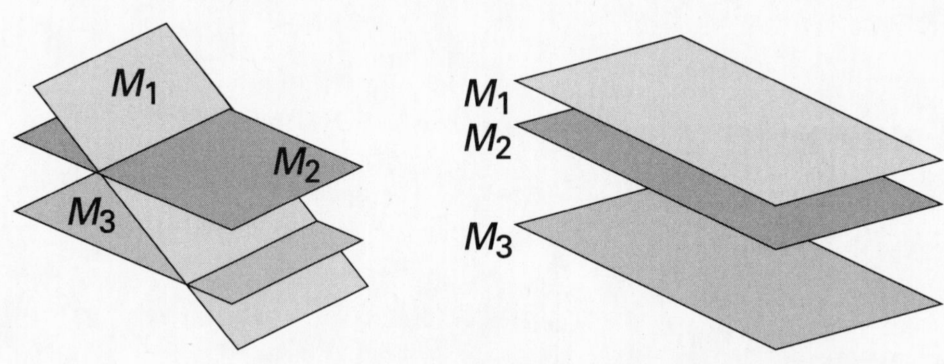

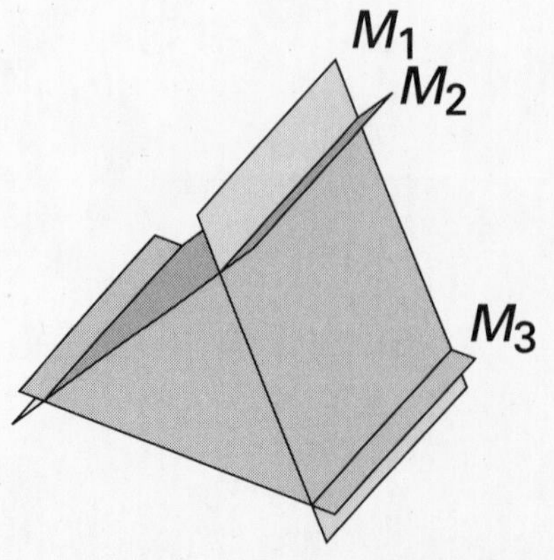

Warm-up

Lesson 13-1

A polygon has vertices (0, 0), $(a, 0)$, (a, b), (c, b), (c, d), and $(0, d)$, where a, b, c, and d are all positive.

1. If $c > a$ and $d > b$, what is the area of the polygon?
2. If $c < a$ and $d > b$, what is the area of the polygon?
3. If $c < a$ and $d < b$, what is the area of the polygon?

Warm-up

Lesson 13-2

In 1–3, find the value of the multiple of the series shown.

1. $1(1^2 + 2^2 + \ldots + 10^2)$
2. $0.5(0.5^2 + 1^2 + 1.5^2 + 2^2 + \ldots + 10^2)$
3. $0.25(0.25^2 + 0.5^2 + 0.75^2 + 1^2 + 1.25^2 + \ldots + 10^2)$
4. What might be the next sum in this sequence?
5. How is this sequence related to the reading of Lesson 13-2?

Warm-up

Lesson 13-3

On page 799 of the Student Edition, upper and lower Riemann sums for $f(x) = \sin x$ are pictured. Six intervals are used to calculate each sum, and each interval has length $\frac{\pi}{12}$.

1. Using a calculator, find the values used to calculate the number 1.12518 found for the upper Riemann sum.
2. Using a calculator, find the values used to calculate the number .86338 found for the lower Riemann sum.

Warm-up

Lesson 13-4

Consider the finite sequences
$a_1, a_2, a_3, \ldots, a_{10}$ and
$b_1, b_2, b_3, \ldots, b_{10}$.

Suppose the sum of all terms of the first sequence is S and the sum of all terms of the second sequence is T.

1. What is the sum of the sequence c, if for all i, $c_i = a_i + b_i$?
2. Write the results of Question 1 using Σ-notation.
3. What is the sum of the sequence d, if for all $i, d_i = 5a_i - b_i$?
4. Write the results of Question 3 using Σ-notation.

Warm-up

Lesson 13-5

In Lesson 13-5, the area bounded by the x-axis, the line $x = 1$, and the parabola $y = x^2$ is shown to be $\frac{1}{3}$. Use this result.

1. Find the area of the region bounded by the y-axis, the line $y = 1$, and the parabola $y = x^2$.

2. Find the area of the region bounded by the y-axis, the parabola $y = x^2$, the line $x = 1$, and the line $y = 4$.

Warm-up

Lesson 13-6

Each of these figures can be thought of as a surface of revolution. Name a possible generating curve and describe its relationship to the axis of revolution.

1. Sphere

2. Hemisphere

3. Cylinder

4. Torus (doughnut)

Warm-up

Lesson 13-7

Name several functions f that satisfy $f'(x) = 2x$.

Distance as Area

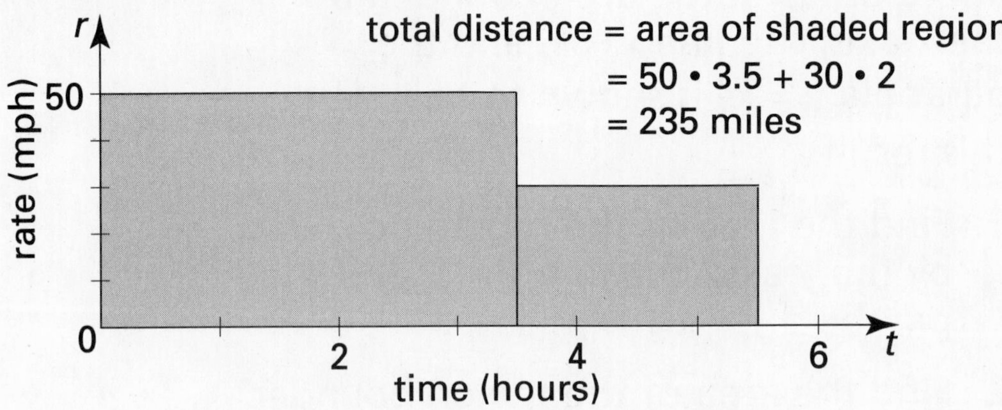

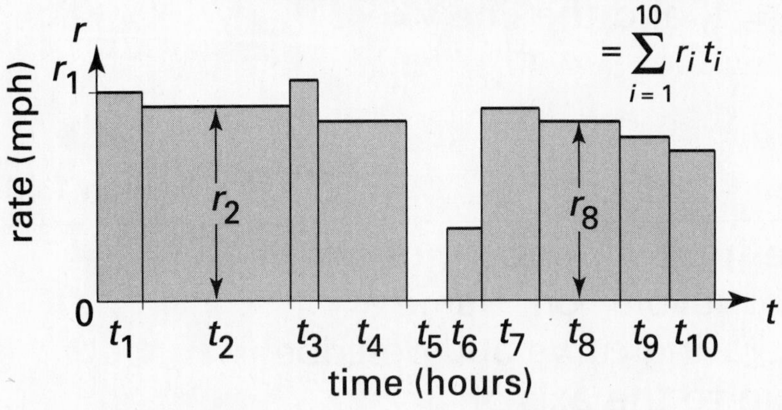

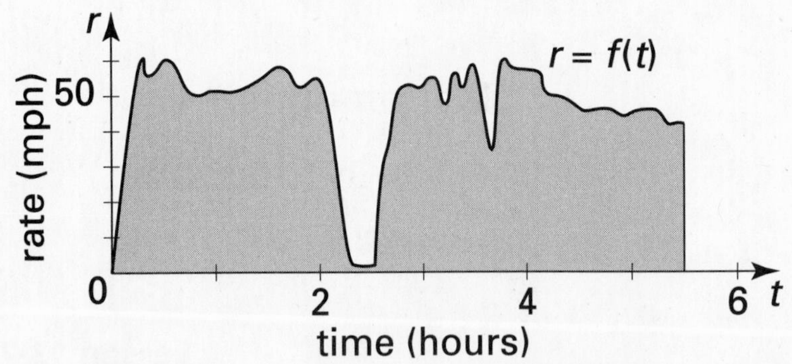

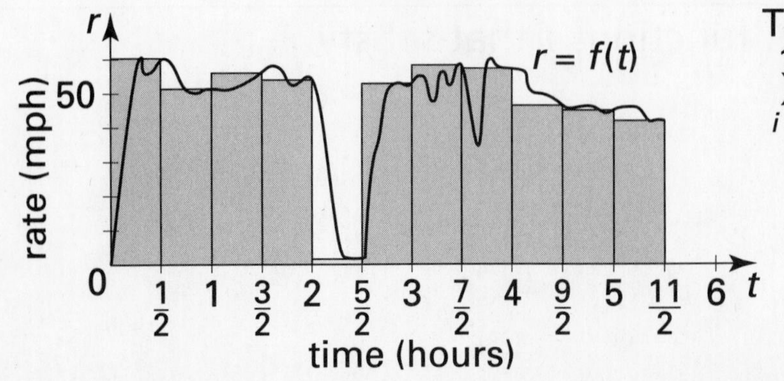

The estimate is $\sum_{i=1}^{11} \frac{1}{2} f\left(\frac{i}{2}\right)$

Example 1

$$g(x) = -.88(x - 10^2) + 88 \frac{ft}{sec}$$

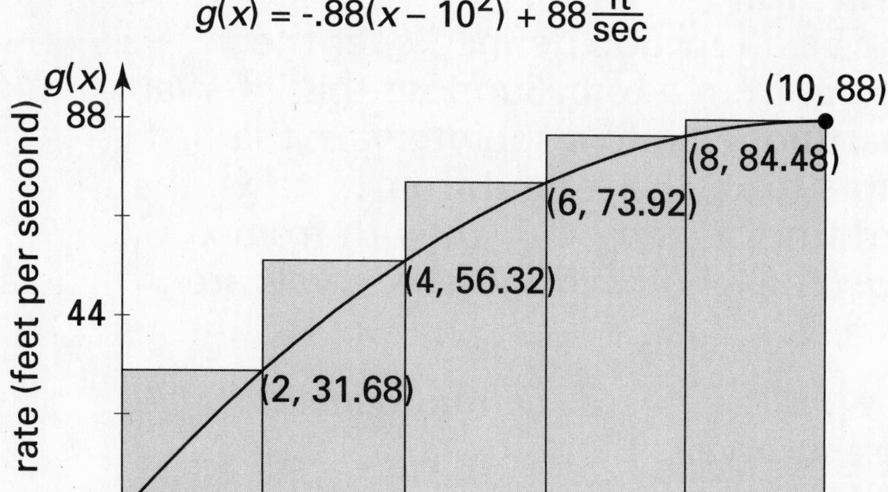

Example 2

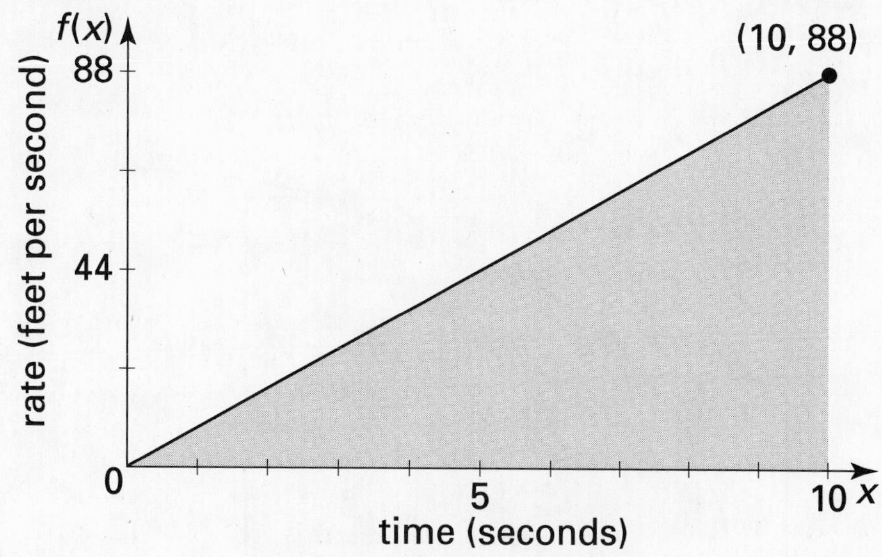

Definition of Riemann Sum

Definition

Let f be a function defined over the interval from a to b. Suppose this interval is partitioned into n subintervals: the first from a to x_1, the second from x_1 to x_2, the third from x_2 to x_3, . . ., the nth from x_{n-1} to b. (The lengths of these intervals are $x_1 - a$, $x_2 - x_1$, $x_3 - x_2$, . . ., $b - x_{n-1}$).

Let $z_1, z_2, z_3, \ldots, z_n$ be numbers in these intervals. Then $f(z_1)(x_1 - a) + f(z_2)(x_2 - x_1) + f(z_3)(x_3 - x_2) + \ldots + f(z_n)(b - x_{n-1})$ is a **Riemann sum of the function *f* over the interval from *a* to *b*.**

By letting $x_0 = a$ and $x_n = b$, then Riemann sum above can be written as

$$\sum_{i=1}^{n} f(z_1)(x_i - x_{i-1}).$$

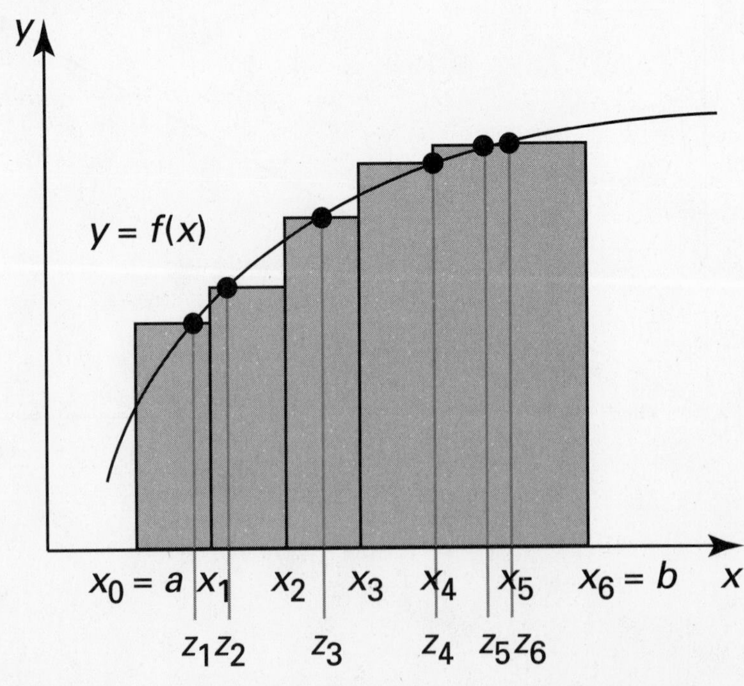

Questions 5, 12, and 16

5.

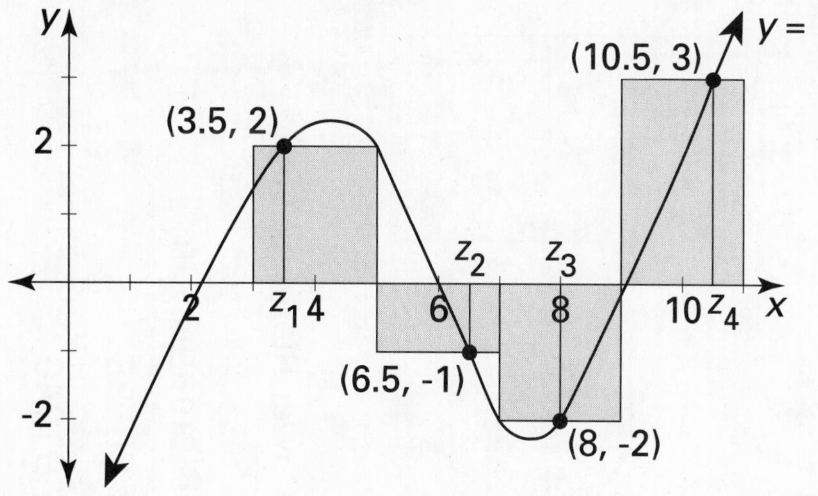

12.

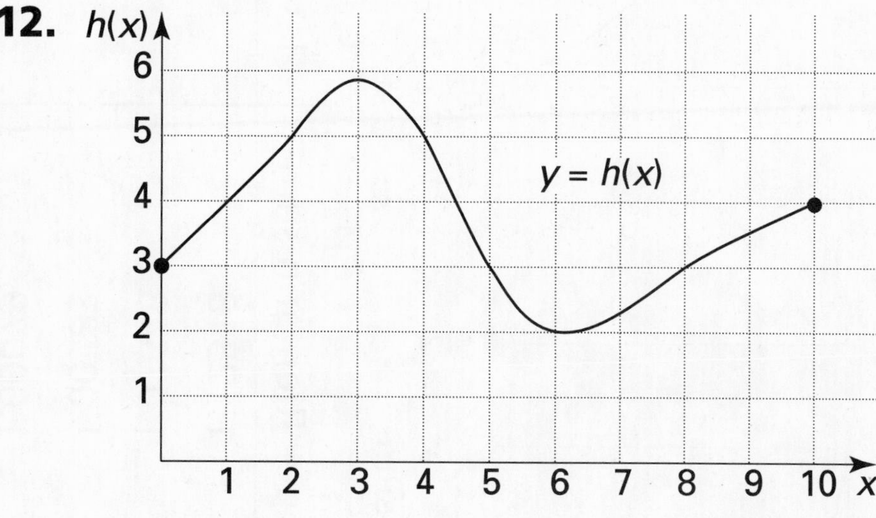

16.

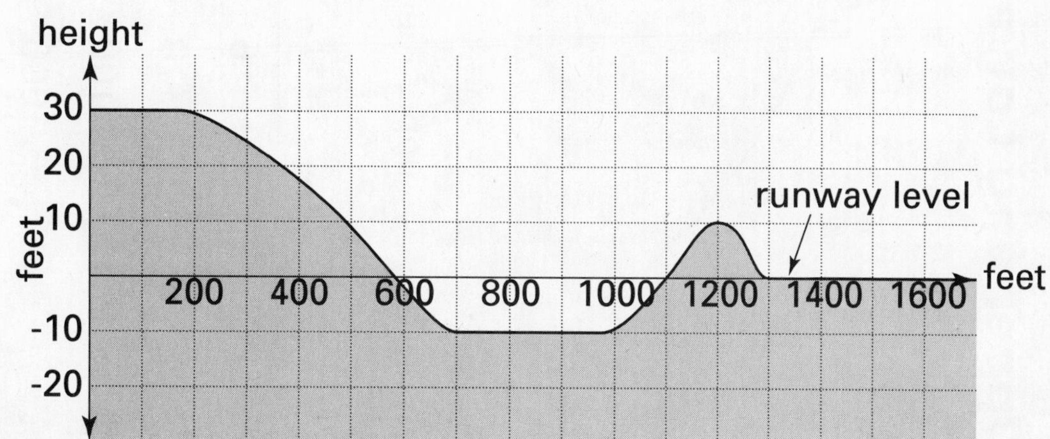

Upper and Lower Riemann Sums

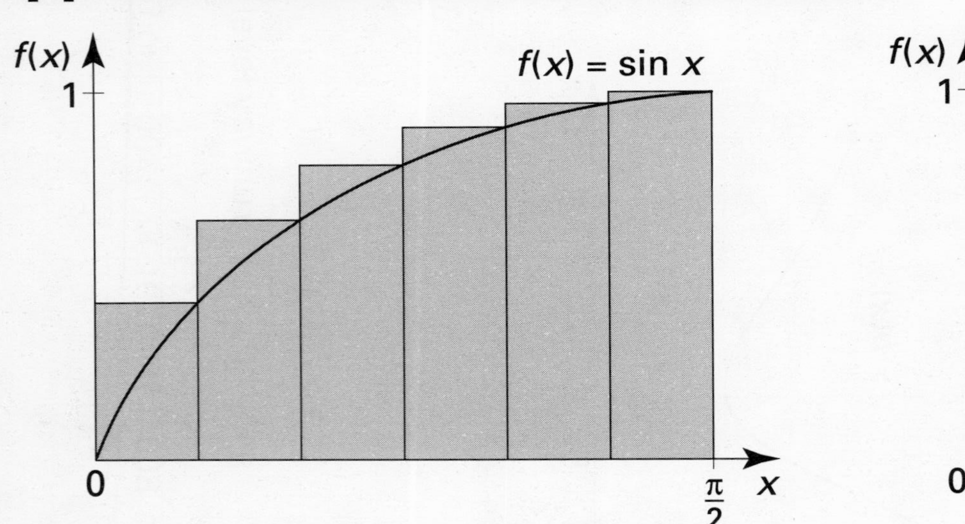

upper Riemann sum

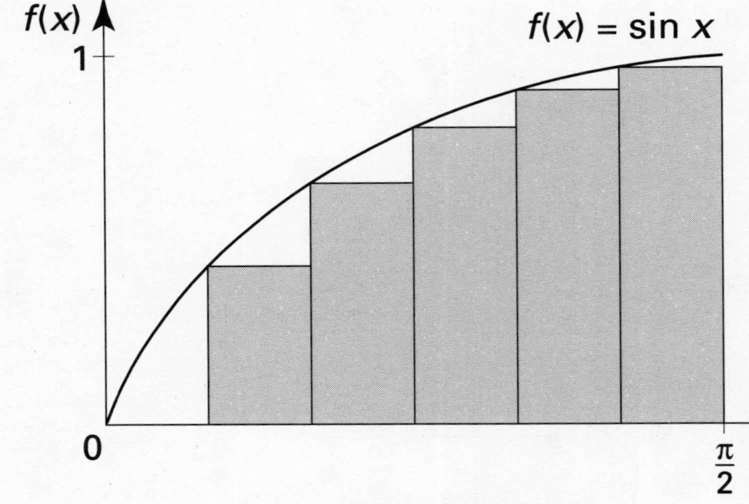

lower Riemann sum

N	upper Riemann sum	lower Riemann sum
6	1.12518	.86338
10	1.07648	.91940
100	1.00783	.99213
1000	1.00079	.99922

Examples

Example 1

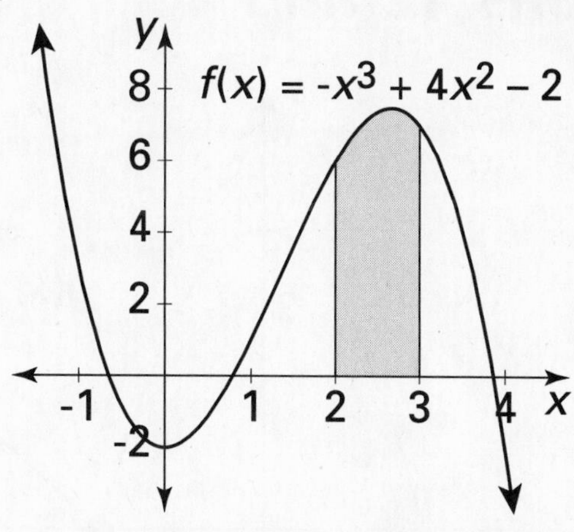

Example 2

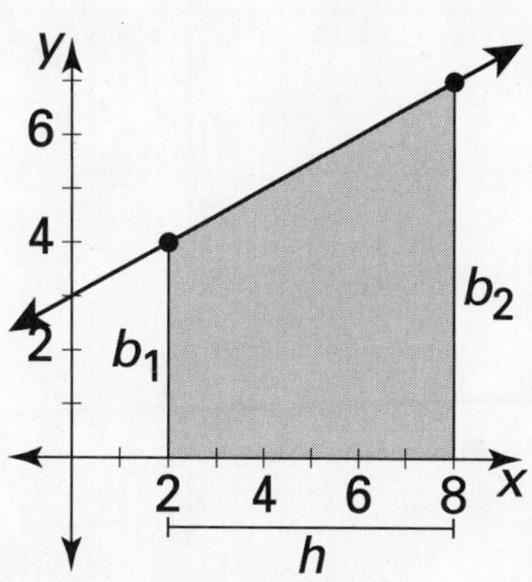

Example 3

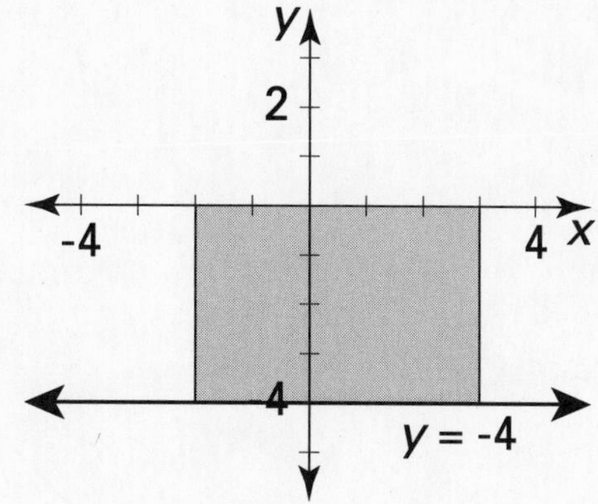

Example 4

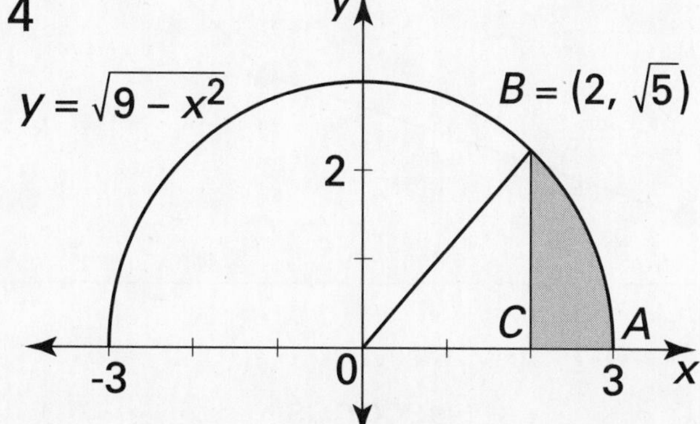

Questions 12 and 14

12.

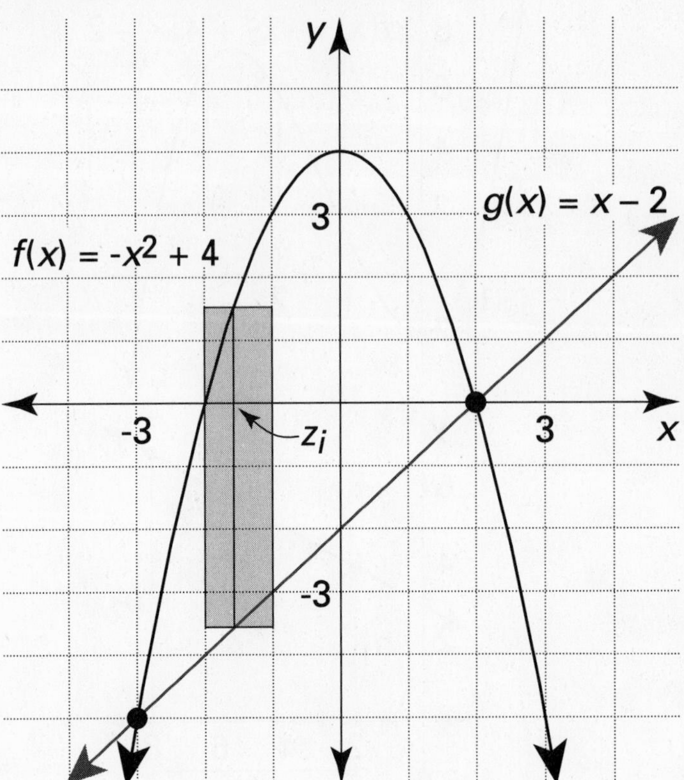

14.

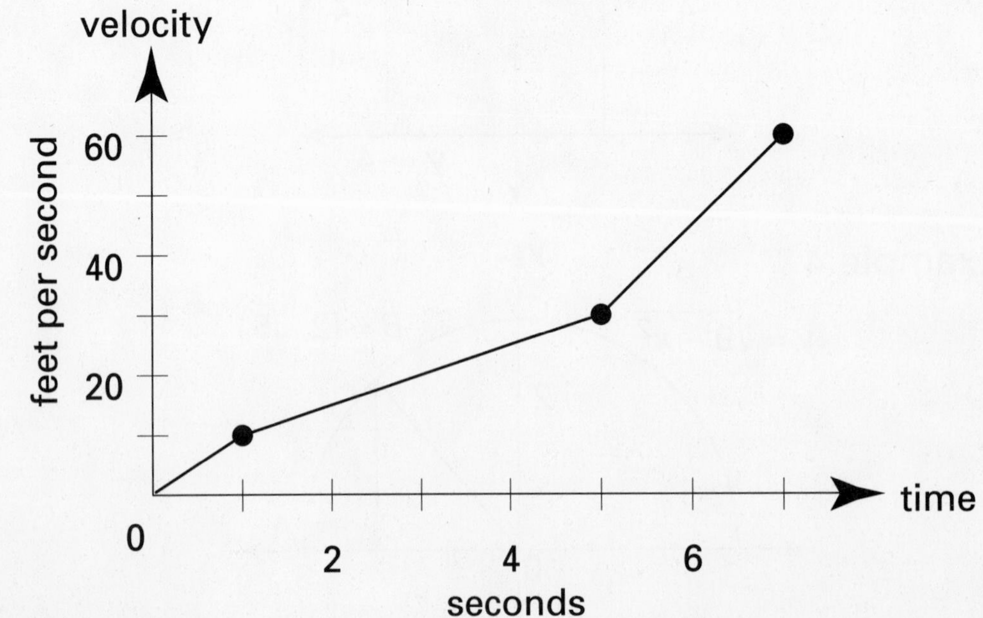

Graphs of Parabolas

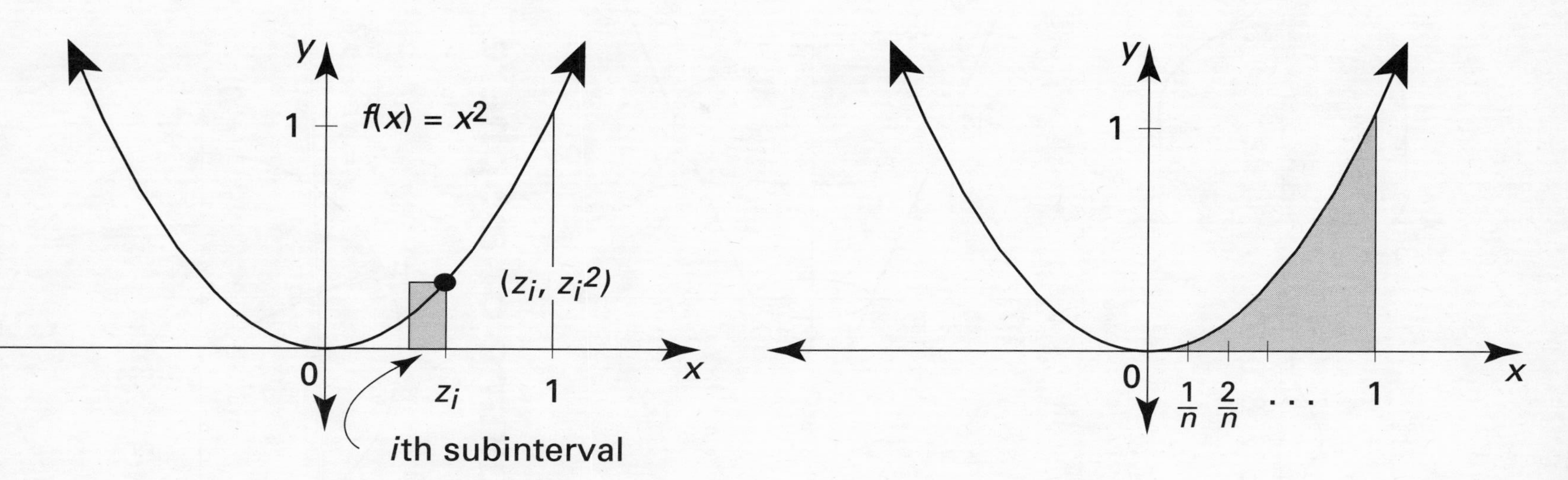

Example 1

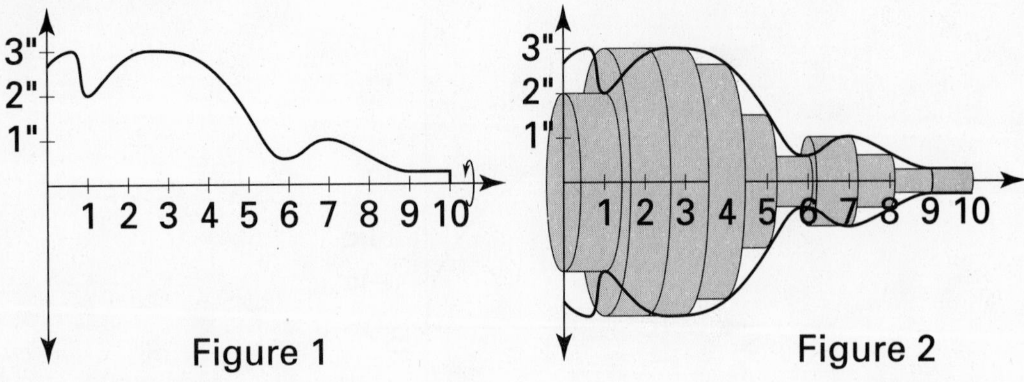

Example 2

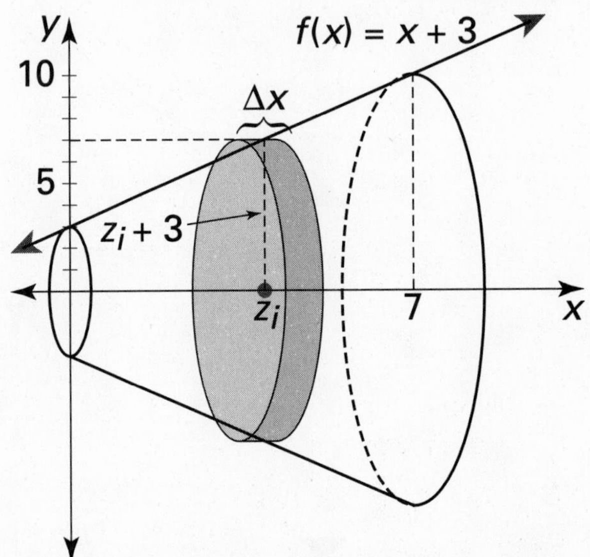

Proof of Volume of a Sphere Theorem

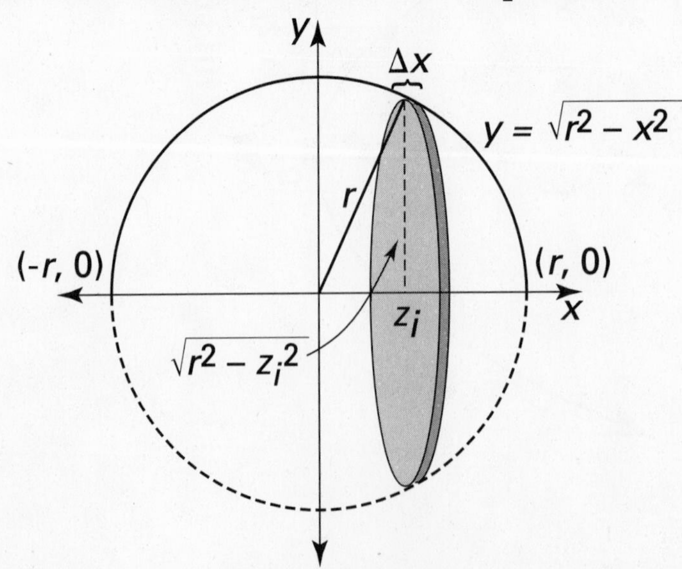